WRITING ABOUT OBJECTS

WRITING ABOUT OBJECTS

Crafting Nonfiction From Things

Melissa Tombro

BLOOMSBURY ACADEMIC
LONDON • NEW YORK • OXFORD • NEW DELHI • SYDNEY

BLOOMSBURY ACADEMIC
Bloomsbury Publishing Plc, 50 Bedford Square, London, WC1B 3DP, UK
Bloomsbury Publishing Inc, 1359 Broadway, New York, NY 10018, USA
Bloomsbury Publishing Ireland, 29 Earlsfort Terrace, Dublin 2, D02 AY28, Ireland

BLOOMSBURY, BLOOMSBURY ACADEMIC and the Diana logo are trademarks of Bloomsbury Publishing Plc

First published in Great Britain 2026

Cover image: Seamless flower pattern © mrs.kato / Adobe Stock

A catalogue record for this book is available from the British Library.

A catalog record for this book is available from the Library of Congress.

ISBN: HB: 978-1-3505-1829-2
PB: 978-1-3505-1830-8
ePDF: 978-1-3505-1831-5
eBook: 978-1-3505-1832-2

Typeset by Deanta Global Publishing Services, Chennai, India
Printed and bound in Great Britain

For product safety related questions contact productsafety@bloomsbury.com.

To find out more about our authors and books visit www.bloomsbury.com and sign up for our newsletters.

CONTENTS

Introduction 1

1 Introduction to Nonfiction Object Writing 7

2 Personal Collections and Collecting 39

3 Autoethnography and Research 65

4 Public Objects and Collections 83

5 Things We Leave Behind 109

Conclusion 139

Additional Student Examples 147

Bibliography 195

Index 198

INTRODUCTION

What Is This Book?

This book is intended to prepare writers to think about the objects in their lives so they can successfully write about them. In the following chapters, I will help you consider the objects you are surrounded by from both personal and cultural perspectives. Creative nonfiction and qualitative inquiry writing practices are explored alongside interdisciplinary subjects to inspire you to create engaging, reflective prose. My goal is for this book to be as user-friendly as possible. I offer a range of topics, assignments, and examples of writing to be used as inspiration for your own work. Many creative nonfiction books and essays have been written with the focus on the object for storytelling. Object writing also reaches far beyond creative writing and spans a multiplicity of fields and genres. In this book, I hope to give an overview of some of this history of and the possibilities for object writing in one unified volume.

Who Am I?

I am a third-generation antiques dealer as well as professor of English at an Art, Design, and Business school. From the time I was brought by my parents in a banana box at 3 days old to an antiques auction, objects have been central to my life. I both hate and love them, sell and collect them, hide them away and revel in the nostalgia they can evoke for my own history and times I have never known. I grew up in a house filled with fine art and antiques. My parents bought and sold antiques for a living, and I spent weekends doing flea markets with my grandmother.

I am intimately connected to objects and eerily detached from them at the same time. It is a rotating cycle when you are involved in resale—love and hate, accumulate and throw away. Antiquing is something I've never stopped doing.

This book comes from my complicated love for things and what they can inspire in us. I have been teaching and writing creative nonfiction for over 20 years. I have written about objects creatively and academically, while always encouraging other writers to use physical materials to inspire their prose. I found myself looking for a book to use to help my students benefit from interdisciplinary creative nonfiction object exploration. I never found one that did what I needed, so I decided to write one myself. On our journey together, I will share my own research, curriculum, personal stories as well as the stories of my students in order to show you the possibilities for real-life object writing.

Beyond my personal and pedagogical experiences, my point of view is informed by my work as the developer and coordinator of Women and Gender Studies at my home institution. As a curriculum developer, I create coursework to help students identify how implicit and explicit biases and experiences shape how we view our world. You will see more research reflecting these ideas as we move into qualitative inquiry and institutional collections.

This book will primarily consider a US-based perspective on objects and their valuation. This perspective is due to the fact that I am based in New York City, where I have been teaching and conducting research for the past 20 years. Additionally, throughout this book, there are global examples of object valuation and cultural influence on object perception. Because this curriculum comes from an interactive class setting that is based on students' immediate surroundings, most writing examples and field trips shared here have their basis in New York City. That being said, I have made the assignments and laid out exercises so that they can be adapted to your home countries and communities. In fact, this work encourages writers to embrace what surrounds them, from personal spaces to the homes of friends and family, individual towns, and cultural institutions. The great thing about object writing is that it can be done by anyone, anywhere, and it is most interesting when each person's personal and cultural experiences are represented.

What Is Object Writing and How Does It Benefit Us?

People live their lives surrounded by objects. Increasingly, individuals focus their lives on the acquisition, accumulation, and worship of items to an extreme degree. Humans can be interested in things for so many reasons, ranging from their monetary value, the memories they hold, the thoughts they inspire, the skills they showcase, to what they communicate to others. There is a wide range of reactions to the objects in our lives, and we can find great satisfaction from buying, keeping, and even purging all that we have. As a species, we create things simply for the pleasure of having them, and we create and collect them in an excessive amount that can lead to our own destruction. From entertainment to advertising and social interactions, we constantly consume and share narratives about objects and what they should and should not mean to us.

Despite our attachments to materiality, many creative writers get lost in a kind of philosophical thought about their lives. They wax poetically and unpoetically about feelings or memories and get caught summarizing experience rather than indulging in the specific. Concreteness is always a challenge for the writer. As any storyteller knows, capturing the right example can do the work for you. Specificity is the key to universality, and capturing well-chosen details and scenes on the page improves our ability to connect to our audiences. Objects can help us achieve these goals.

With the consideration of objects, the writer is able to work through a number of issues relevant to creative writing and cultural analysis. This book focuses on the power of materiality in storytelling, the setting of scene, the social nature of objects and collections, the extremes of society, and how we come to understand ourselves and others based on what we and others own, value, and discard. In particular, the work with qualitative inquiry, institutional collections, and refuse is essential for writers who want to extend their scope outside of the self and into the larger cultural sphere.

My first book, *Teaching Autoethnography: Personal Writing in the Classroom*, has been widely adopted for first-year writing courses because of its emphasis on the critical capacity of personal writing in the classroom. This book makes the same case from a different point of view—as we move past rigid ideas of research and structure, we see the potential for critically understanding the world through personal writing in new ways. Objects allow us to latch onto writing in ways that more rigid ideas of research and production limit. This curriculum provides a route for conversation with the world around us, which includes literary, artistic, and cultural perspectives. This approach is equally valuable in our creative writing classrooms and our personal lives.

There are many directions one can take in the consideration of objects. This book is not meant to comprehensively present a history of object theory and writing. Rather, this book draws from interdisciplinary exploration and writing practices to create an approach that is accessible and relevant for writers of creative nonfiction inside and outside the classroom. In the following chapters, I will provide writers with information and assignments to effectively consider the art of nonfiction object writing in order to craft stories of your own. I provide detailed overviews of a number of different object writing topics and share assignments that can be used to improve your own personal writing. I share my overview of creative nonfiction pedagogy as well as applicable qualitative inquiry methodology. Included in the chapters are an overview of relevant texts, my own ideas on the separate topics, suggested readings, writing assignments, personal memoir, case study examples from my environs in New York City, and student examples. I have broken concepts down into some general categories to help us move through in a logical way. These topics move from personal considerations to cultural understanding of objects and their value. Our first topic is collections and collecting, followed by autoethnography and gender, institutionally collected objects, and finally objects left behind. All categories are imperfect and tend to overlap. The intention of these general categories is to bring together concepts to help us understand what we value in our own personal lives and broader communities. With these different elements, I hope to inspire readers to consider their own history with things in order to tell good stories.

In order to inspire high-quality writing, writers have to be able to critically engage and attach themselves to the subject matter, and that may look different for each person. Examining why people collect objects, why objects inspire us to write, and how we can translate these ideas into prose are all part of the book. Good thinking leads to good writing. Qualitative research is a tool to push us to see past initial observations into the value of personal cultural examination of attitudes and practices.

Throughout this book, the case studies from sites I have visited on my own and with students are presented to inspire writers to think about spaces and objects in them in their own communities as inspiration for their writing.

What I will examine in the following chapters shows how, as individuals and as a society, the things we value send powerful messages about identity. Special objects can inspire imagination and evoke admiration and even jealousy. Common objects can tell stories of daily life and relationships and even show our inner selves. What is collected can be a source of pride or shame, and what is discarded demonstrates what we value and what we do not. I hope to demonstrate how creative nonfiction writing can help us to examine the cultural and personal significance of objects. We will consider how writers can come together around common cultural objects and refuse, as well as why individuals and institutions collect things and how our relationships to and views of these collections can inspire storytelling. Topics and ideas covered include but are not limited to: collecting and collections, cultural and monetary value of objects, family history and nostalgia, gender in relation to objects, public collections and archives, inherited objects, garbage and recycled objects, objects and status, generational trends and fads, and objects in the age of social media. These topics are an outgrowth of my experiences and of the spaces and students I teach. I encourage you to expand these topics to fit your own goals for your writing.

How to Use This Book

I have organized my chapters in a way that readers can feel free to engage exercises individually as a writer, or use the book in its entirety for a semester-long course in creative nonfiction or arts-based writing. I have used all of these assignments in diverse classroom settings and find that they can augment and improve the writing process on their own. Each chapter is designed to stand alone and the assignments related to the topic are contained within the relevant chapters. Depending on the goals of the reader, a few of these assignments might inspire a singular piece or an entire journey. There is no right or wrong way to make use of the information found here. I have included a student example from my classes for each assignment as well as an appendix at the end of the book with additional student examples. These will give you a clear idea of what can be accomplished within the confines of a semester.

Included in the chapters are eleven assignments—seven what I call informal "Low Stakes" writing assignments which are unrevised and done within a week, and three what I call formal "High Stakes" writing assignments which go through a long 3-week revision process. When writing, it is important to have a mix of Low Stakes and High Stakes assignments. The informal writing assignments allow us to engage ideas and meditate on objects without too much consideration for the quality of the written projects. The larger revised assignments allow us a multi-tiered process where we can draft and share pieces in peer workshop and get feedback from your professor in order to get more deeply into your ideas and writing process. Each piece of writing is considered in group discussion, but taking inspiration from the Amherst Writer's Method, unrevised pieces are treated gently and with positive feedback only. I will describe the application of this point of view when I give an overview of pedagogical considerations in Chapter 1. There are more assignments in later chapters by design. As you become more familiar with the topics and more practiced with the writing, there are more assignments on each topic to deepen your connection to the material and push you further into complex reflections.

1 INTRODUCTION TO NONFICTION OBJECT WRITING

Starting Off Together

On the first day of class, I introduce a general question—what is an object, and why would we write about it? I will post this question on the board and invite students to engage in a freewrite. For our purposes, a freewrite means we put pen or pencil to paper (I like the mechanics of handwriting for in-class work) and free associate on the topic. We write for 10 minutes without a break and try to just keep writing without overthinking it. If we get distracted in the writing, we push through and try to find our way back to the topic. This pause in the beginning of class gives us a way to see what organically comes up in relation to the topic. Students might be considering why they signed up for the course or what their expectations are. They may write about things they like or how they've been taught to consider objects in their lives and schoolwork. We share our ideas from this writing out loud to get a conversation started about what our expectations are for class and how we can work together to explore these themes. I will try to help you do that throughout this book—why are you reading it? What do you want to get out of it as a student? As a writer?

Our classroom structure encourages students to storytell in order to better understand their relationships to objects. I believe as a professor it's important for me to engage in this work alongside my students in order to build an open and trusting classroom community. For this reason, I share my personal stories with my students. I will also share my own creative writing in this textbook so you can get to know me and my relationship to objects. The following is a sample of my writing from a longer memoir that explores some of my earliest memories in the antiques business. Throughout this book, I will continue to share small pieces of my writing and student writing for the same purposes, so you can get to know us as people and object writers.

Personal Memoir

The market surrounds me from the time I wake up—early morning, I huddle underneath my hospital cornered bed sheets freezing because I am never able to set them free and curl them around my perpetually icy toes. Grandma turns on the light, 3:15 am, clockwork, and I wiggle under the tight flannel trying to shield my eyes from the dresser lamp.

She begins her routine by opening the top left drawer under the horizontal mirror. I often look in this drawer when she is in the other room. Filled with neatly arranged coral lipsticks, blue mascara and eye pencils black/brown worn and soft. The smell from a dozen tiny bottles of 30 year-old perfume fills the space with a well-cared for nostalgia—the same routine, the comfort of wear, the smell of memory. Sometimes when I can't coax myself back to sleep I watch her through half open eyes—Aqua Net tall and slender filling the room with a dank haze, lips smacking and lining eyelashes short and coated. Her sweetness in waking me up made me hate her. "Rise and shine lazy bones."

A 1950s print of Jesus with two little children hovers above my head as I pull down a pale rose chevron knit blanket made from a scratchy familiar acrylic. This one and the one on the twin bed beside me were made especially for me—"You can keep them." I would never want to. The chill in the house is abated by a pair of house slippers and a robe that always make me look lazy in comparison to my meticulously made-up grandmother. My knee length hair, wavy and light brown gets me the nickname Gravel Gertie when I wear it down. Instead, I tie it neatly in a bun, how I will continue to wear it until I cut it off when I am 25.

The brown shag carpet cuddles my feet and my layers are already laid out for me on the chair. This is better—up until last year, Grandma and I would share the bed she slept in with my grandfather. After he died, I would sleep on the right side of the bed she on the left, curled up on her side while the loud long buzzer of the 1960s alarm clock and imperceptible staticky radio woke us up in the morning. Wrapped in plastic, a pillow my sisters had embroidered for my pop-pop laid on the freshly made bed. Every day she would say the same thing, "I am so cold, you are my hot water bottle." As I migrated to the twin bed in the other room Grandma did indeed heat her hot water bottle again.

Undershirt, blouse with a collar, corduroys, sweater, wool socks, laced shoes, go. Thermoses of hot chocolate filled the car for our arrival—tiny cups of coffee and Entenmann's by the side of my pillow as I dozed on the car ride there. When I was young, I would try to stay awake, and as I got older I would doze off to Engelbert Humperdinck—the only tape I ever bought my grandma and thus the only one she ever played.

I have driven this route many times in my life, passing road signs and early morning truckers in the dead of night, dozing when I was and wasn't actually behind the wheel. From the highway to the farm fields that stretch before us on the edge of the Delaware River we hug the mountains doing the speed limit. On the left a stretch of headlights and dim lamps ease us onto dusty gravel and the same spot my grandmother has been parking on Sundays for 30 years. We never drive alone—my great aunt drives to meet us in the dark, the same way she has since they first started the market with my grandfather years before. She tails us in her maroon Rabbit all the way to Pennsylvania where we settle into our spaces next to each other and next to Jose.

I hide in the car and watch as my grandmother takes out her neatly pressed blue bed sheet tablecloths and spreads them on the warped brown wooden tables to claim the space. The banana yellow umbrella that will shield us from the heat of the summer sun beating down on us at midday is neatly secured to the table with a metal hoop. Two rusty folding tables that weigh more than I do are set out front to hold my Barbie dolls, jewelry, and glasses that I sell throughout the day. I sit wrapped in a blanket on a stool, with my tiny cup, my cake and my small stack of bills that will grow over the hours until it is a large mass in my pocket that I fondle with pride.

At age six I know the drill, never back down, don't bargain, learn how to read the customer. Reading people and knowing what people want is the trick, judging how much they want it and what they are willing to pay for it. It is a transferable talent that leads me to know what people want to hear and how I can benefit. It's never how much something costs it's a balance of disregard, friendliness and banter. I make friends, growing up among an array of characters that both scare me away from and invite me into their world. I feel more at home here than I do anywhere else and my first love becomes the grimy dust-colored objects that I carefully pack and unpack every week in their newspaper and banana boxes. I am home.

Personal Memoir Analysis

In this piece, I explore a core routine that defined my early experiences doing the flea market with my grandmother. I set up a booth with her for many years after my grandfather died when I was 6 years old. I was her companion, and we would shop for antiques together and sell them on the same weekend. Here, I try to establish my relationship to the business, my grandmother, and my surroundings so the reader can feel situated in my experience. While the writing focuses on objects, I use some of the trappings of creative nonfiction writing that I will explore in this chapter to make sure my audience feels that they are part of my story. I try to provide enough information about my circumstances and point of view so my reader can make a connection with me. It doesn't try to cover everything about my long history with antiques, and I don't employ every consideration in creative nonfiction. Instead, my writing offers insight into a singular repeated experience when I was a child: learning how to run a small business of my own alongside my grandmother.

In the following sections, we will explore why authors write about objects, look at the first assignment from my class, read a student example, and go into some stylistic considerations that are important for writing object creative nonfiction before going through tips for workshopping our writing together.

What Do We Learn Through Writing About Objects?

Many theoretical books have examined why we have an increased fascination with objects and writing about our connections with them. Object interaction encourages us to use the five senses to unlock memories and ideas. According to Severin Fowles in his essay "People Without Things," which examines the "turn toward things in social theory" (Fowles 2010: 38),

> The recent focus on materiality . . . can be understood as a response to a world reduced to discourse, filled with unstable meanings that have been cut free from anything solid or unproblematically "out there". It can be understood, in other words, as a corrective to certain strands of late twentieth century social theory in which the real seemed to be lost in the hyperreal and in which the world was left feeling a bit like shadows and fog. The result has been a remarkable interdisciplinary effort to raise the status of *things*, to tip our hats to their agentive presence in the world, to explore their hidden materiality, and to expose the powers they command. (Fowles 2010: 24)

Essentially, we are hungry for things we can touch and experience firsthand. We engage them more intentionally and thoughtfully to help us think through our lives. By engaging with material things, we can more comfortably expand into abstract thought and exploration. Fowles's ideas can be used to help us consider our attachment to materiality as a way to ground our understanding of the world and our place in it.

Popular media showcases people's histories and fascination with important objects in their lives. From day one in class, we analyze why objects are so important for storytelling. Many of us already use objects to tell our own life stories and to show others who we are. This sharing may not be through formal writing; it may be in casual conversations and interactions, in posts on social media, or via the images we send to friends and family. The sheer number of things that can fall into the category of object, and the large range of ways we already interact with things, can be overwhelming to explore. In this section, I will take us through some of the sample readings I use in the beginning of my class so we can start to understand possible subjects and outcomes for object writing.

Beyond theoretical texts, early shared readings in class help us understand how authors have already done important work using objects as a basis for writing. *In Short: A Collection of Brief Creative Nonfiction*, edited by Judith Kitchen and Mary Paumier Jones, is a manageable collection of essays about stuff that gives samples of the short form creative nonfiction I am encouraging you to write. It does not show authors who have done heavy theoretical work with the writing or even advanced plotting of narrative. Rather, it shows a wide range of smaller pieces that get at the heart of a relationship with things in a quick and interesting way.

When *In Short* was published, I was a college student myself, grappling with how to write and tell stories. Short-form nonfiction was not very popular and the genre itself was still being defined. Kitchen and Paumier Jones speculate about the rise in popularity of the short nonfiction genre and the purposes it serves for the writer.

> We don't pretend to know why all of a sudden so many diverse writers are writing Shorts. We can only offer some tentative speculation. Twenty years ago a nonfiction piece one or two pages long would have been extremely rare, a book with a two-page chapter unheard of. Writers felt obligated to set the scene, develop the plot, and provide the transitions. Today, writers skip or condense much of that, and readers, schooled by the quick takes of television and movies, translate what they have learned there to the written page. Writers take advantage of that, further schooling readers, and on it goes. We see the development of the Short as part of that wider cultural trend, and as one part—one fascinating part—of the experimentation in the burgeoning field of what is coming to be called "creative nonfiction." (Kitchen and Paumier 1996: 23–4)

In today's world, we may extend the idea of quickness to include posts on social media from Instagram to TikTok. Capturing impressions and quick reflections is a great way to start off the writing process.

Our weekly informal class writing can be categorized as short-form nonfiction since it is meant to be a snapshot, a brief and meaningful understanding of an object. I encourage you throughout your writing to copy down impressions and initial responses to small items in your lives. Writing down quick impressions of things surrounding us is a nonthreatening and Low Stakes way to regularly engage in inquiry about objects. Engaging Low Stakes writing assignments for ourselves invites us to simply notice and start recording thoughts without worrying whether what results on the page are worthy of publication or even further exploration. Through this book we will build a practice of inquiry, where reflecting and noticing will allow more formal pieces to emerge. Some of the longer formal writing naturally evolves from these short pieces if my students find there is more to probe. Other times, these pieces are just what they are, ways to practice noticing that might lead them to also figure out where they really want to spend time on extended and revised writing.

Some essay collections combine theory and brief writing in order to go deeper into the meaning of the objects for the writer. Stories are connected to theoretical exploration which can add to a writer's understanding of how we can connect these ideas to a world beyond the page. Sherry Turkle's edited collection, *Evocative Objects: Things We Think With*, showcases a wide-ranging group of shorter writings by interdisciplinary authors who want to understand the importance of things in their lives. In the introduction, Turkle begins by recounting her own childhood relationship to objects and then explaining the value for the authors included. The power of connection through materiality rather than the mechanics of an object is a central theme of the book. "Evocative objects bring philosophy down to earth. When we focus on objects, physicians and philosophers, psychologists and designers, artists and engineers are able to find common ground in everyday experience" (Turkle 2007: 8). Organizing the writing in a series of categories, Turkle emphasizes that it is through conversation that these pieces help us think through the bigger issues in life. "These texts begin to describe the kinds of connections that help us investigate the richness of objects as thought companions, as life companions" (Turkle 2007: 9). This is a good way to start thinking about the things in your life—what is important and not important to you? How did it get to be that way? How do you understand yourself in relation to the things you surround yourself with? Do these things connect you to others? Separate you from them?

In its Object Lessons series, *The Atlantic* gives an opportunity for writers to explore their relationships to objects such as,

> the hidden lives of ordinary things, from sardines to silence, juniper berries to jumper cables. Each Object Lessons project will start from a specific inspiration: an anthropological query, ecological matter, archaeological discovery, historical event, literary passage, personal narrative, philosophical speculation, technological innovation—and from there develop original insights around and novel lessons about the object in question. (https://objectsobjectsobjects.com/about/)

There aren't limitations on the topics or the background the author has for this series, which includes articles as well as short books. I like to introduce some of the shorter pieces in class to help students think through contemporary journalistic examples of how a material thing can have a much larger meaning for the holder. There are a number of pieces I use from the series, some that I will share here, to start off class discussions about object writing.

In "The Secret to Good Writing: It's About Objects, Not Ideas," John Maguire discusses his work as a college writing instructor and how he helps students understand their abilities as writers by getting them to focus on the materiality of the things in their lives. "No matter how abstract your topic, how intangible, your first step is to find things you can drop on your foot" (Maguire 2012). It is helpful for us to remember as writers that this kind of return to the physical and material is something that has been employed by teachers and writers for many years. While it is not a new idea, it is one we can deepen through exploration.

In "A Birth Certificate Is a Person's First Possession," by Christine Ro, we begin to consider how a piece of paper can come to define a person and who they are and what liminal space they occupy in this world. "The birth certificate becomes the first object most people own. Bound up in official identity and personal relationships, its stakes are high" (Ro 2017). This is a great example of what the lack of an object can mean. If you don't own a birth certificate, it can determine the course of your life. What your birth certificate says and where it comes from can affect myriad aspects of your future.

In his book for the Object Lessons series, *Souvenirs*, Rolf Potts talks about souvenirs which he defines as, "objects that are collected for personal reasons during the course of a journey" (Potts 2018: 7). In his first chapter, he explores cheap knickknacks related to the Eiffel Tower that are sold at countless stores in Paris. This might be a familiar sight for any of us that have visited the city or any major metropolitan area where there seem to be endless stores full of useless crap. People flock to the establishments in order to try and capture their visit for themselves or for their loved ones who could not make the trip themselves. "In a sense, souvenirs are a metaphor for how lived experience can endow most any object with personal significance" (Potts 2018: 9). These mass marketed items have little meaning of their own, but buying them on our travels changes their importance. Since I teach in New York City, this is a productive discussion as we are surrounded by endless shops that have pieces related to the Empire State Building, the I Heart NY logo, One World Trade Center, and the Statue of Liberty. Even if you don't live in a tourist hotspot, almost anyone can see this even in the smallest of hometowns where shops and even chain stores have come to sell countless generic items with town names, historic sites, and even sayings that would appeal to those visiting.

In these collections and examples, we start to see a lot of ideas about storytelling and pedagogy and the types of inquiry that are considered valuable from the serious and simple topics that can be explored under the umbrella of objects. The goal is to lead us into asking questions about objects in a general and accessible way. We can use theory to consider objects and we can read the stories of others to understand experience. Starting with a question or simply picking an item that is important to you can help you begin to understand your relationships to things. I will give an example of a first-round assignment inspired by some of these ideas later in this chapter to get your writing started.

Creative Nonfiction Pedagogy—A Brief Introduction

In this section, I will provide some practical Creative Nonfiction Writing pedagogy that you can apply to the ideas in this book. While there are countless volumes exploring the various definitions of creative nonfiction, for our purposes it is writing that is meant to interpret and present true events in a creative and reflective way. I actively discourage you from focusing too much on the mechanics and ideas behind good writing before diving headfirst into the initial assignments. Giving writers the freedom to engage objects in any way they see fit helps me as the professor understand their point of view on the topic and also get a feel for their writing in a more organic way. Similarly, I encourage any user of this book to let go of their ideas of good writing and rather engage in good thinking to get to the heart of what the objects they are examining mean to them. This will allow you to truly connect to the subject matter without attaching too much to outcomes. This is the same reason I assign writing that has no drafts and writing that has multiple drafts. There is time for ideas to be developed into good writing, but first you have to have a good idea! So just go for it!

Please remember: it is rare that writers employ all of the suggestions below in a single piece of writing. My hope is that the following sections will set up some ideas for you to consider as you develop your personal writing style. I would suggest referencing this chapter as you build your writing portfolios.

Establishing Trust

At the start of class, we spend the remainder of the first day after introductions discussing two concepts of central importance in the writing of creative nonfiction: the twin issues of truth and trust. As a writer, establishing trust with your audience through truthful storytelling is key to communication just as it would be with a friend or colleague you are trying to connect with. Unlike other forms of writing, we are intimately reliant on things being real and true in creative nonfiction, and on this basis, we form our attachments to the stories. Any story can have the potential to unlock feelings and attachment, but nothing does this quite so well as something that is supposed to be true. It is why in real life we feel so betrayed when a friend or partner lies to us. It may be a big lie or a small lie, but our trust and thus our relationship can be easily shattered by an untruth.

In class, I often share the story of James Frey's *A Million Little Pieces*. There was a huge public outcry when The Smoking Gun website revealed that this bestseller contained embellishment and lies. As Oprah had recommended the book for her book club, she took it upon herself to first stick up for Frey but soon after invited Frey on her show to make him take accountability for deceiving her and the public. "Winfrey began the live program by telling him, 'It is difficult for me to talk to you because I feel really duped. But more importantly, I feel that you betrayed millions of readers'" (https://www.history.com/this-day-in-history/oprah-winfrey-takes-james-frey-to-task-for-lying). Here we see a popular example of what it means to break trust with readers with rare publicized consequences for doing so. Refunds were offered by the publisher to all who purchased the book and Frey was made to apologize. "Frey's fabrications sparked a national debate over the definition of memoir. In the aftermath of the controversy, he was dropped by his literary agent, and his publisher settled a class-action lawsuit brought by readers who claimed they had been defrauded. Future editions of *A Million Little Pieces* included a note from Frey in which he admitted to altering parts of his story" (https://www

.history.com/this-day-in-history/oprah-winfrey-takes-james-frey-to-task-for-lying). After this intense backlash, fact-checking in creative nonfiction was amped up to avoid future fallout. It doesn't matter that the majority of Frey's writing was based in his experiences, the lies he included made his literary achievement and his trust with his readers null and void.

As writers, we may expose the complex lies and truths connected to objects, but we ourselves don't want to deceive our audiences. Instead, we want to weave interesting stories and maintain our ethical beliefs while entertaining our readership. While we are not able to fact-check most of life, there are keys to keeping our writing as honest as possible. In the following section, we will think about what establishing truth actually means in terms of our own writing.

What Is Truth for the Writer?

I begin any discussion of creative nonfiction writing in class with a central question—what is the truth? Students are immediately wary. This is not a philosophy class, after all, but we still need to contemplate our core values when writing nonfiction and establish what our relationship to memory and facts should be.

For our purposes, telling the truth means representing something accurately to the best of our ability. There are countless stories of memoirists being outed as liars for fabricating moments and stories, like Frey above, and lawsuits coming from people because they feel they are misrepresented on paper. While it is interesting to look at those examples and see how impactful they were to the people affected, it is most important to establish our own understanding of truth in writing while also trying to meet the expectations of others.

Mimi Schwartz in "Memoir? Fiction? Where's the Line?" talks about her experience as a teacher and what it would look like if we didn't explore truth for ourselves. She explains that it's the emotional truth that is most important. It is one of my favorite passages, so I will share it at length.

> Go for the emotional truth, that's what matters. Yes, gather the facts by all means. Look at old photos, return to old places, ask family members what they remember, look up time-line books for the correct songs and fashion styles, read old newspapers, encyclopedias,

> whatever—and then use the imagination to fill in the remembered experience. You don't need a tape recording of what your parents said to "remember" what they said that day. You don't need a photo of your kindergarten teacher to describe her; the clothes you imagine will match your feeling about her. Maybe you see a red, mini-suited girl; maybe you seen a woman in a thick, long black dress with white cuffs. Either way, we see the teacher as you saw her. And who knows? She might even have worn those white cuffs! The subconscious is remembering. (Schwartz 1998: 36)

In the Schwartz excerpt, we can see an emotional interpretation that allows us to get to the reality of events and histories. We don't have access to a visual or auditory record of most memories, so we have to do the best with interpreting the importance of the events for us through the evidence that we have.

A similar idea holds true for Joan Didion in her famous essay, "On Keeping a Notebook," where we are taken on a journey about her expansion and interpretation of reality. In her essay, she recalls how she is even called out by family members over her differing interpretations of memories and questions her own ability to tell true stories. In the end, she justifies this exploration simply, "*How it felt to me*: that is getting closer to the truth about a notebook" (Didion 1968: 23). An understanding of the feeling we take away from an interaction or experience is what we want to communicate to our readers.

To broaden these concepts of truth, we can look to Toni Morrison. In her essay "The Site of Memory," she explains, "The crucial distinction for me is not the difference between fact and fiction, but the distinction between fact and truth. Because facts can exist without human intelligence, but truth cannot" (Morrison 1998: 193). As she writes here, truth is about coming to an understanding about what the facts mean and represent. Everything is based on perspective and this is what leads us to coming up with a perception of events as they happened. Truth for all of our writers relies on consistency and a certain amount of accuracy but is ultimately about understanding something larger about our experiences while being as close to the facts as possible.

For most writers, there are a few different rules to follow that can allow you to remain as truthful as possible in your creative nonfiction. While it is good to rely on our emotional reality, we want to make sure to stick to facts as much as possible for our readers. Here are a few tips and questions to ask yourself to keep things as truthful as possible:

1. If you are discussing another person in your story, would you show them this story? Why or why not? This can reveal where you feel you have been overly harsh or not quite accurate for storytelling purposes. Nonfiction is about real people, so it's important to think that those people could care about how they are represented.
2. When writing dialogue, we will not be able to recount every word exactly as it was spoken. Does the style of speech and intention of the words remain intact? Is it consistent with the voice and characters of the person speaking?
3. In a scene, we have to be honest about what we remember and what we don't. Can you do your best to share details of what surrounds you? Can you use the five senses to recreate a moment? When that fails, always admit when you don't know and when you are not sure. We always trust someone who is layered and complex more than someone who pretends to be perfect or comes off as one note.
4. It is important to always also remember that the author gets to choose what they share. Being truthful does not mean pushing past our own boundaries. The wonderful thing about writing our own stories is we get to decide what we write about and how we write about it. Don't let anyone pressure you to share things you do not want to. That is not necessary for good writing.

I had a good opportunity to publish a memoir at a young age. I intended the memoir to be about my life in the antiques business, but publishers and agents were more interested in the death of my father, which plays a part in this story. For me, it was not the book I wanted to write, and that's okay. Something can be part of our story, but we may not want it to be the focus. We have to be true to ourselves.

In "To Fashion a Text," Annie Dillard drives this point about choices home. "The best memoirs, I think, forge their own forms. The writer of any work, and particularly any nonfiction work, must decide two crucial points: what to put in and what to leave out" (Dillard 1998: 143). As you go more deeply into the writing process, you should feel free to use your best judgment to decide how you will pick both content and form.

Now, in the following sections, I will break down some of these concepts alongside some basic creative nonfiction pedagogy in more detail to help you on your writing journey.

Starting the Formal Writing Process with Objects

A writer cannot write about the self without a certain amount of self-esteem and a healthy ego. If we don't find ourselves interesting, nobody else will either. We need to find what is intriguing in our own lives and how we can invite others into our stories. Many of us have been pressured to mine our lives for importance and have been led astray into writing about topics that we might not find joy in exploring. Understanding what is "significant enough to write about" can be confusing.

It is not surprising that as a student you might think back to college essays when considering what to write about. It got you into college, didn't it, and it is most likely the most time and effort you've spent polishing a piece of creative nonfiction. You might also harp on what teachers, friends and family, and even popular culture and social media have told you is best or most interesting about yourself. We are all victims of this. We are sensitive to the messages from those around us. We tell stories about ourselves because we are expected to, but they may not be the best stories or even the truest.

All of us also have additional stories we tell again and again. These can be tried-and-true tales that have impressed friends and acquaintances. These stories may be our go-to moments that explore times when something outrageously good or bad happened to us. They may contain a series of crazy coincidences or come to a tidy conclusion. When we tell a story repeatedly, it can sometimes feel stale and seem distant from real experience. The narratives we think are the most extreme are often not the most interesting for our reading audiences.

Sometimes we need to get these stories out of our systems because they are blocking our access to other ideas. It is okay if you start with some of these narratives, but most likely you will find later in your writing journey that they are not the stories you find the most satisfaction in having told. Allowing ourselves to move beyond these well-worn narratives is essential to our growth as writers. I actively discourage writers from limiting focus to their most familiar stories in my classes. I want them to focus on moments that are small and seem relatively unimportant to them in the grand scheme of things. These stories should hold interest for them, but I don't want every topic to have a forced sense of value. I want them to liberate themselves from who they think they are or should be. As writers, it is important to expand our scope to reimagine what is suitable for writing and how we can access these ideas. Using objects is a great way to reframe what makes for an interesting topic. Interacting with physical things brings us out of our own heads and patterns and lets us breathe new life and meaning into our writing.

I have had so many students express how freeing it is to not have to establish their value on personality traits, identity markers, or accomplishments. Rather, they love having the ability to write freely about their emotions and attachments, serious and not. Often, in taking the pressure off of themselves to continue the narratives that got them where they are today, they find out a lot about themselves in a natural way through the writing and exploration. The process of considering the way they value the objects in their lives allows their writing to progress naturally into meaningful storytelling.

By simply observing our lived experiences at the start of this journey, we find we are surrounded by material that says a lot about us and the worlds we inhabit. Taking a look at what you keep in your bedroom is a great way to start, and that is the topic for the first assignment I give students in class. Below, I include the assignment and a student example.

This assignment would be written soon after the considerations above. The ideas following it would not be discussed until this first piece of writing is completed. I will use this assignment as a way to demonstrate how one of my students used some basic creative nonfiction techniques in her writing. While I will not analyze student writing in this book, in the following sections, I give some writing advice that will help you make the best use of the assignments that follow our introductory chapters. I encourage you to visit the student examples throughout the book to consider how these different ideas can be used to their full effect in your own writing.

Assignment and Student Example

Assignment #1 (Informal "Low Stakes")—Bedroom Objects

For this week, you need to choose an object from your bedroom space that tells a story of who you are and then tell that story. This item needs to be available to you now and portable as you will need to bring it to class where we will use it for another writing exercise. Your writing should be one to two pages double-spaced, closer to the 2 mark. You will be sharing these pieces with the rest of the class.

Intention of the Assignment

The way I open up the discussion of object writing is by having students look at what is most readily available to them. It is important that it occupies an intimate space that they have some control over. For most students, who live in dorms or at home, that space would be a bedroom. The use of the bedroom can work for anybody because it is a space where we keep fewer extraneous objects and quite often things that we consider more valuable to us. It is not uncommon for students to explore a piece of jewelry, a picture or artwork, greeting cards, diaries, stuffed animals, or tchotchkes that they like to keep close.

This is an informal assignment meant to open us up to understanding how what we choose to surround ourselves with can tell a story. It is a way to reveal a bit of ourselves to the class as we get to know each other.

For my purposes, I like students to choose something accessible and portable. This makes this assignment a bit like show and tell. I have students bring the object to class and put it on a shared table. I then invite other students to choose an item that intrigues them from that table, pick it up, and write what they think of it and to reflect on why it might be significant to one of their peers. We do the writing part in the form of a freewrite, pen to paper, for 10 minutes. After the freewrite, each student shares what they picked up and why they thought it was interesting. This is followed by the writer sharing what the object means to them. We compare the perceptions of the chosen object.

This demonstrates how our own life experiences and perceptions can determine how we view something. It is always interesting to see how students' valuations of objects overlap and sometimes greatly differ. It shows how much value in an object is intrinsic and how much is assigned by the owner or the observer. We discuss how shared backgrounds come into play and how cultural and generational signifiers might lead peers to understand the object on a certain level. We learn context is key to perception. This simple assignment usually yields rich discussions that make everyone consider their relationship to stuff in a fun and interactive way.

Student Example Assignment #1—Bedroom Objects

Hailey Duffett—Virginia Is for Lovers

Florida is the "Sunshine State". Missouri is "Far from Ordinary". And "Virginia is for Lovers"; which makes it the perfect possible state for me to have grown up in. A naturally positive person who really just likes to smile, this cheesy slogan is my perfect connection to home. So I bought a postcard off of eBay, thinking that it would just be cute to put on my wall for some dorm decor. Once my parents had begun their trek back to this state that was so perfect for me all that I was focused on was spending the night perfecting my dorm room. I cleaned, talked to my roommate about posters and collages, and got to work decorating the room. But when sticky tacking this postcard to the wall I was struck by the sudden realization that I was no longer in this perfect state. Where are all my people who also live by "Virginia is for Lovers"? My thoughts regarding this postcard launched me into a small breakdown. Sitting on a stiff bed I wallowed in the inconsistency and uncomfortability of this new state.

At 42,774 mi^2, I would be lying if I said that I know the state of Virginia like the back of my hand. Even when traveling far distances for field hockey games in high school sometimes an hour drive felt like it had taken us into a foreign country. But the county of Alexandria, right below DC, quite simply was my stomping ground. Best ice cream? Trail? Coffee Shop? Cheapest sushi? Farmers markets? No one could match my expertise.

I have attended a small private school my entire life. Surrounded with the same friends from kindergarten all the way to my senior year, my extended family lived nearby. I never once moved houses, and as I said before really knew every spot to fulfill whatever I wanted to do at any time. What I am trying to emphasize is that my life was extremely consistent. I was never really forced to experience much change beyond puberty and the completely inconsistent Virginia weather. Living in this perfect little environment, I had everything that I could ask for, so how could I not be a "lover", the perfect Virginian. I loved my area and everything in it so of course I show this quality to others. I will hold the door, I will always try to meet someone new, volunteer; the whole nine yards. I will do my very best every day to spread love.

So you can imagine the genuine shock to my system leaving this curated little county. When moving here two weeks ago, I genuinely felt like I could take on anything. I listened to all the New York songs; I was so ready to be an uptown girl. The drive into the city didn't feel like I was leaving home, it felt like I was about to take on New York City. I was so focused on what was in front of me I didn't turn around. But once I was sitting in my dorm room, all that I felt was like I was a Virginian lover who had been displaced. With no more of this consistent and comfortable lifestyle I began to comprehend how out of my element I was. I honestly had a hard time. Where were my friends? Where is the cheap sushi down the street?

But after about a week of going on walks and beginning to orient myself the slightest bit, I realized that although all of my surroundings are shifting and different from what I am used to, what is consistent is my loving nature. Me, Hailey Duffett, is the exact same. I still hold doors, make conversations, and now I am in a new place and can do all of these things for new people. A postcard on my bedroom wall is what made me realize I was away from home on the first night and now is a daily reminder of where I have come from and who I am. I am a "Lover" all the way from Virginia and that is all that I need, my attitude and care. The story that this postcard tells about me is one of how I am just beginning to comprehend the time of transition I am in and feeling a connection to home and myself every day.

Stylistic Considerations for Creative Nonfiction Object Writing

Why Are You Telling the Story?

This is something I say in every one of my creative writing classes, and in my first book I call it "who cares." In other words, why would somebody want to read this? Why do you want to tell the story other than the fact that you are being asked to by your teacher? If you don't see value in something, there is little chance that your reader will. As I mention above, we need to reframe what has value. Try to think about what those in your life might want to hear about and the kinds of topics that you find personally interesting. Your topic doesn't have to be a big, life-changing takeaway moment. That being said, it should be something you'd find joy or satisfaction in exploring with a friend or family member.

While we all want to please our imagined or real audience, we must find motivation beyond simply fulfilling a task in our writing. Besides, we can never really please everyone. Perhaps we don't know why we want to share our story, but we feel compelled to. Perhaps we want to write in order to explore something that we can't articulate verbally. Maybe we have a passion that we want to put into words. Even if we are writing because we have to, we want to ask ourselves why we have made the decision to write about this specific thing. The exploration of that question will yield interesting results for you and the reader.

Context

I am certainly not the first writing teacher to tell students that context is key. But what does it mean to provide context? An object without any referent holds much less meaning than objects within a well-defined literal and mental space. We see this in Assignment #1 when Hailey looks to her own past through the objects on her wall. Consider other examples: what does it mean to look at an antique necklace in a box without context? It may be beautiful, or valuable, or show the style of its era and wearer. If you learned that the necklace was actually worn by your grandmother when she first came to this country and got married, you might feel more complex feelings toward the object. We like to know who is telling us the stories and why, and this in turn gives our subject meaning.

In a class, students can get used to the nature of the teacher/pupil relationship. The context is that they are taking this class for a grade and their teacher ostensibly knows who they are. I try to break away from this idea of context and how we as writers must consider readers outside of the classroom in multiple ways. I love to use common everyday examples in order to do this as I will demonstrate below.

Audience and Self as Authority

When we talk to a friend or family member who knows us very well, we don't have to provide certain kinds of information. They know a lot about our history and our personality. For instance, it would be weird to start a story off with your best friend by establishing where you grew up and how you came to go to college. It would be equally strange to talk to a parent you grew up with about how and where you were born. This means the first lesson about context is audience.

For most of us, only a small handful of people will ever read our writing. Some of them will definitely be friends and family or our teachers who know and support us. But what about people we have never met? How can we make them understand us and care about what we have to say?

If you are trying to make a new friend, you might tell them some of the things mentioned above to give context for who you are and where you are coming from. Depending on the person and circumstance, you will most assuredly share different kinds of details and information that you find appropriate or relevant.

Make a friend with the audience. What do you think they would need to know about you in order to understand and value your point of view? This can be a trial-and-error kind of experience. We don't always get it right in person, and we won't always get it right on the page, but we have to try to think outside of ourselves to understand what the reader needs to know to keep reading! (Because that's the point, right?) How cool is it when someone reads what you've written and goes, wow, I never thought that before, or this made me think of my own life or see something a different way? Writing is a way of connecting with others, and context is key to establishing that relationship.

We can't understand as readers what we are supposed to get from a story unless we know who is telling us the story and why. The use of personal detail to establish who the writer is and why they are sharing this is essential. A little can go a long way.

Other People

When we include other people in our writing, there are a few key things to consider. What does their presence add to the story? What do we need to let the reader know about them to establish the importance of their presence and voice?

We have discussed how to establish ourselves on the page through giving context, and it is important to do the same with other characters as well. You need to provide enough information to the reader so we know who the person is and where they are coming from. If you don't want to spend time on the page doing this, it is a clear sign that this person is not important to your story.

When trying to recreate a moment in time, we might be inclined to include everybody in the room. Most writers of creative nonfiction do not do this. They pick and choose which storylines to follow and who to include based on what relationships are most important to the narrative. The reader will get lost trying to follow a bunch of strangers they do not know on the page. Often, in full-length memoir, we might never realize our main character has siblings or parents because they are not mentioned. This does not mean they are being untruthful. It's simply an important lesson; we should only include people and relationships that matter to the story we want to tell.

Consistency Is Key

With writing, consistency is key because nonfiction writing is based on the idea of trust that we explored above. We want readers to trust us and see things from our point of view. To do this, we have to maintain an approachable writing voice that takes in the messiness of life. This is the opposite of what we might think, that consistency means making sure there is no complexity.

In everyday life, we rarely trust people who are prone to extremes or come off as one note. We may find them amusing and even seek them out when we are in a particular mood, but we don't find them to be as trustworthy. Do we trust anyone who is happy all the time or whose life is a constant non-stop drama? Not usually. The far ends of the spectrum in terms of personality can be amusing or needed but overall make most people wary.

Real life is full of ups and downs. We have good days and bad days. We may have a predisposition to certain personality traits, but in general, we find reality and personality to be complex. This means our writing needs to be complex and it needs to consistently take a complex point of view to be trusted. Our writing is just one possible way to understand something and that is okay. Nothing is ever definitive. By being true to our own complicated natures, we are showing the reader who we are.

Scene and Setting—Getting the Details Right with the Five Senses

Being able to place objects in space is an important skill for writing. I encourage students to do this as much as possible. I try to explain that the focus on materiality in this class necessitates showing the material conditions in which they are viewing the objects. These settings can be as simple as their room at home and as complex as the maze of a public garden or halls of a museum.

Use of the five senses is important in recreating space as it is in recreating the allure of the object. For most sighted people, we may become overly reliant or privilege visual cues when our experience is truly informed by so many more of our sensory experiences. For a student writing about a favorite stuffed animal, they might consider the following: where the animal is placed, the smell of the room, the feel of the animal, the smell of the animal (good and bad, and how we find comfort in gross and used things and smells comes up quite a bit in this context), the look and feel of the room, other objects in the room, the temperature, the sounds of the space, and taste where appropriate (consider a child who chews on their favorite childhood blanket and then smells it). All of these ideas about scene and more are relevant to our understanding of the objects.

In *The Art of Memoir*, Mary Karr focuses on the idea of carnality to discuss how she teaches the use of the five senses. She explains,

> Carnality sits at the root of the show-don't-tell edict that every writing teacher harps on all the time, because it works. By *carnal*, I mean, can you apprehend it through the five senses? In writing a scene, you must help the reader employ smell and taste and touch as well as image and noise. The more carnal a writer's nature, the better she'll be at this, and there are subcategories according to the senses. A great glutton can evoke the salty bite of pastrami on black rye; the sex addict will excel at smooth flesh; the one with a painterly eye visual beauty, etc. Every memoir should brim over with the physical experiences that once streamed in—the smell of garlicky gumbo, your hand in an animal's fur, the ocean's phosphor lighting up bodies underwater all acid green. Of all memoir's five elements, carnality is the most primary and necessary and—luckily for me as a teacher—the most easy to master. (Karr 2015: 71)

It is no coincidence that Karr is a fan of object writing. As she continues her discussion of carnality, she focuses on the importance of things. "The great writer trolls the world for totemic objects to place on a page. In every genre, it's key" (Karr 2015: 72). Keeping these lessons in mind, she shares the reaction she gets from her readers when she writes a particularly vivid description of an object. "Strangely, readers 'believe' what's rendered with physical clarity. I once had a reader say, 'I knew when you put in that old can of Babbo cleanser you were telling the God's honest truth'" (Karr 2015: 74). It is the ordinary nature of the included object and the specificity of it that reads true to the reader. "Of course, physical details, however convincing, actually prove zip in terms of truth" (Karr 2015: 75). While these details may be truthful to our experience, they are not evidence of anything. The key to understanding Karr's point here is to acknowledge that details are important for a reader trying to connect to a story and an author.

This plays into something I always communicate to my students: it's in the details that we capture our audience. Sometimes we believe that by being more general we are more likely to get readers interested in our stories when the opposite is true. The more specific we can be to our experience and the more details we can share, the more likely someone will identify with what we are saying. Think about this when we share stories with friends or family—the more we are able to set the scene, the more invested they become in what happened. Who hasn't felt the smack of recognition when reading a book as seeing something beloved from childhood or so ubiquitous from an era we are nostalgic for?

Dialogue

It is hard to feel confident that we are accurately portraying conversations and people when we try to recreate dialogue. Writing nonfiction is a careful balance of memory and interpretation. We want to do our best to accurately represent the spirit of dialogue in a consistent and ethical way. Despite our sometimes complicated feelings about recreating conversation, using dialogue in our storytelling is important. It gives the reader an opportunity to decide for themselves what people are like by hearing them through their own words.

Most people do not like to be spoken for or to have their words misinterpreted. Think about real-life frustration when someone speaks over you or tries to anticipate what you are going to say next. Letting people in our stories speak is key to giving up control of the narrative and letting the reader in. It frees us from constantly interpreting someone else's words and lets the reader decide what they feel the words mean.

Most of us do not remember long discussions in detail. We may have a feeling for the overall arc of the conversation or an impression of the tone and meaning of what was said. For this reason, most writers of creative nonfiction do not try to recreate long moments of dialogue between characters because it seems false. While there are some writers who do write out lengthy exchanges, such as Jeannette Walls and Lucy Grealy, for our purposes it is best to consider what you want the reader to take away from another person's words and to use dialogue effectively and sparingly. Less is more. A well-chosen line can show us a lot while a long conversation can distract from the purpose.

I often ask students to do an informal dialogue exercise where they recreate a real-life conversation they had with another person. It has to be a real conversation, and it has to be a spoken conversation (no writing involved in the initial conversation so that they don't rely on text to make up for memory). Something needs to happen in the conversation, but it doesn't need to be something big. They are instructed to recreate the conversation, only between them and one other person, without giving any explanation of the lines. During the workshop, we as readers then need to assess what we see as the relationship between the two characters and what we think happened in the conversation.

The benefit of this informal exercise is that you can't hide behind interpretation; you must let the characters speak for themselves. Doing an extended scene forces you to practice capturing the arc of a conversation as well as your voice and the voice of another character in the story. It makes you look at what actually happened and leave its meaning open to the readers interpreting it. During the workshop, I would suggest staying quiet and offering no context for the conversation to your readers. What others see in the writing can be very instructive, in both good and disappointing ways, and will let you know how well you are communicating with your peer audience.

Here are the directions I use for this assignment:

For homework, please recreate a conversation between two characters, one being yourself. Please write down only the words spoken. This means there will be no explanation of mood, scene, or indications of tone. Choose a moment where we can see something happening in the relationship. There should be, in other words, an outcome of this conversation, large or small.

At the end of the piece, write **one** *sentence where you explain what you think the exchange shows.*

This piece should NOT be based on a conversation that was had without an audio component (FaceTime, in person, on phone, etc.). In other words, don't just cut and paste a text conversation or a recorded conversation. YOU MUST RECREATE THE DIALOGUE FROM MEMORY. Please ***limit the characters involved to two****—you and the other person. Your final piece should be about one to two pages in length, double-spaced, 12 point font. Please post to the discussion board before next class.*

Lots of things will come up when you do this exercise. What does it mean to have something happen over the course of a conversation? How many lines do you remember from conversations you've had? What tends to be the nature of those lines? Why did they stick with you? When you replay that language in your head, how does it make you feel? What insight does it offer you into the person, the nature of the conversation, the relationship, or trying to understand what unfolded in that moment? How does it make you feel about yourself? The other person? The world?

From here, you will want to decide if there are small exchanges or moments that can effectively capture voice and intention without the need to recreate an entire conversation. Good writing is about good choices. Words are impactful—we know this, which is why we write!

As I mentioned in our consideration of truth earlier in this chapter, there is a quick rule of thumb to stay truthful. When writing dialogue, we will not be able to recount every word exactly as it was spoken. Does the style of speech and intention of the words remain intact? Is it consistent with the voice and characters of the person speaking?

If It's Good, You Don't Need a Conclusion, but You Do Need a Title

This speaks for itself—all the good stuff should happen throughout the writing. It needs to be given attention and be allowed room for development, exploration, and complexity. If you feel the need to explain what just happened at the end of the writing, you haven't done the work you need to make the work successful. While not all stories are monumental, they should capture an arc of something happening. We should start at one place of understanding and end somewhere else. Go back, let the journey be reflective and complex from word one, and you won't have to write much of a conclusion at all.

Assigning a title to your work is a difficult task. Consider your audience and what you want to communicate in order to both intrigue your reader and give them an idea of what they will find in your writing. What titles do you respond to and why? In a world of quick internet reading, a good title is all it takes to get us to click.

How to Workshop Creative Nonfiction

Probably the most important part of the writing process is garnering feedback in a trusted setting or from individuals who are sharing your experience. The goal for the workshop is for everyone to feel comfortable sharing what works for them and what needs improvement. In my classroom, we conduct workshops on all Low Stakes and High Stakes assignments. I define workshop as a time for the group to share and respond to work.

At my institution, I teach 3-hour sessions, which I break into halves: the first half is for workshop, the second half is for discussion. For a typical teaching schedule where you meet twice or three times a week, I would devote one session to workshop and one to the discussion of readings. This divided approach allows focus on workshopping the writing as well as allowing time to focus on ideas from readings that will help push our writing forward. If you are writing outside of the classroom, it is great to meet up with friends and colleagues who might also be interested in sharing their work.

Low Stakes assignments are workshopped differently than High Stakes assignments. In the following paragraphs, I will break down goals and methods for each type of workshop.

Low Stakes Assignments

For Low Stakes assignments, or writing that is done week by week without a revision component, I employ elements of the Amherst Writers' Method, as explained by Pat Schneider in her book *Writing Alone and with Others*. Students are asked to choose a selection from what they have written that they find representative of the story to share out loud with the class. Peers are encouraged to take notes as they listen. The most important and only direction I give for feedback is "Absolutely no criticism, suggestion, or question is directed toward the writer in response to first draft, just written work. A thorough critique is offered only when the writer asks for it and distributes work in manuscript form. Critique is balanced: there is as much affirmation as suggestion for change" (Schneider 2003: 187). So for Low Stakes assignments, I provide examples of what they could comment on which include but are not limited to: imagery, description, language choice, topic, ideas, setting, details, storyline, and flow. No critique is invited on Low Stakes assignments as the point is to bond and understand what stands out to others in a positive way. This allows everyone to build confidence in their skills and come to understand what is powerful and interesting about their writing before diving into what can be improved. Sharing out loud can be frightening for writers; this is why everyone shares their work out loud on a regular basis to normalize the process and build a bond of trust with one another.

For Low Stakes assignments, there is no required revision although those writings can be used later on as building blocks for High Stakes, revised assignments. A lot of writers will use the Low Stakes assignments to play with ideas that they will more fully develop in their High Stakes writing. It is equally valuable to explore subjects in the Low Stakes writing that are not directly used in longer High Stakes pieces. The point of the Low Stakes assignments is to have a low-risk way to begin to understand relationships to objects, not to create perfect prose for later development. In fact, it is usually much more challenging to take a piece of writing and expand it than to start fresh. Revision is always difficult, and workshop is a space meant to help us become comfortable sharing work out loud and play with ideas. After this experience, individual writers can decide if the assignment has served its purpose for them or how their work might continue to evolve and grow.

High Stakes Assignments

For High Stakes assignments, we similarly share out loud with one another but also engage in written critique. At this point, I remind students that we are working with real people and real lives, so while we want to help the writer to improve, it is important to remember we are dealing with their feelings and to act accordingly. I give tips for how to balance critique to ensure we are being responsible with the writer and the content. For every part that we think needs work, we must share specific ideas for how it could be improved. For every part that succeeds for us, we must explain how it is working well and why it adds to the piece. By pointing out in equal parts what does and does not work while offering specific suggestions for how the writing is both working already and has potential to be improved, we create a constructive conversation. The reader has to put in a good amount of time and thought into their comments to create a valuable dialogue. We may assume a writer knows what is good, but this is usually not the case. We need to help our peers understand how they are succeeding so they can understand how they can make other parts stronger.

For High Stakes assignments, I require students to give written feedback in addition to verbal feedback for a number of reasons. While we may benefit from verbal feedback in the moment, if we don't have a written record we may forget the valuable comments by the time we have an opportunity to revise. As a reviewer, writing down our feedback also gives us the opportunity to take time and articulate our comments at length without the pressure of immediate verbal reaction. Students do their written feedback in small groups during class. Once they have completed the feedback, they exchange it with their peers who read the feedback and follow up with questions and discussion. This allows for a fully engaged process which leads to more thorough, detailed, and carefully considered revision workshops.

While they conduct peer workshops, I review the pieces as well. After we have completed the process in small groups, students are welcome to ask questions in front of the whole class, and I additionally share an overall impression of the pieces I have reviewed. All students also receive written feedback from me the following week before they begin their revision process.

Sample Workshop Questions

Below is a sample of questions I provide students for written commentary on their Essay #1—Collections, their first High Stakes assignment, introduced in Chapter 2.

Please answer all questions thoroughly on the discussion board so your peer and I can both see the feedback and reflect on it for the revision process. (Our school uses an online Learning Management System for each of our courses.)

1. If you had to sum up the topic of this piece in only two sentences, what would those sentences be? Write them here. (This question encourages students to identify a focus for the piece. If they struggle, this can be a sign the focus is not clear. If they see a focus differently than the author intended, this can be instructive to the author about whether their intentions are clear.)
2. What is the story of this piece? Take me through the events—where they start and where they lead and why. Be specific. (This question asks students to consider the flow of the piece and whether we are taken somewhere from beginning to end. If students are not able to identify a series of events or ideas, it can become clear that there are challenges in the evolution of the story.)
3. Do you know the author as a character from reading this draft? What do you know about them? Is there something you would like to know and don't get to? Please explain. (This question is all about personal context. What do we know about the person telling us this story and why is that important? Does understanding who is telling us the story affect how we can understand the subject at hand?)
4. Who are the other main characters in this piece? List who they are and what you know about them. (This question ensures that any person introduced in the story is explained and explored.)
5. What is your favorite moment in the writing? Why? (This is a direct opportunity to reflect on parts of the writing that work and demonstrate why they work so well for the reader.)
6. What object(s) are the most powerful for you as a reader? Explain and explore why. (I ask this question later in the process because the purpose of object writing is to develop good storytelling. While the object itself is important, it is mostly important as inspiration for exploration.)
7. Which object(s) are the least powerful for you as a reader? Explain and explore why. (It is important to explore if too many details or things distract from the purpose of the narrative.)
8. How does the author use the five senses to explore their topic? Can their use be expanded? Explain. (As discussed above, this is

about how the piece invites us into the setting and context. It is a way to make the reviewer and writer consider how they might add to the feel of the piece or what they are already doing that works well. You want to make sure setting and sensory details are clear.)

9. How do you feel about the title of the piece? Why? (Titling is very difficult and this gives a fun chance for students to have a discussion about what a title indicates for the author and the reader.)
10. Any additional comments? Be detailed! (This is an opportunity for the reader to share any other thoughts or comments that do not fall under the umbrella of my questions. Students are also welcome to copyedit peer pieces as long as they receive permission from the writer before workshop.)

Revision Is Key

Revising our writing can be a painful and frustrating experience. I make sure my students have copious amounts of verbal and written feedback to consider from multiple people for their High Stakes revised assignments. You might be in a classroom where certain standards have to be achieved. Feedback can help you meet those goals. In the larger scheme, the great thing about being a writer is that you get to decide what feedback you want to apply and how to apply it. When my students become frustrated or confused by comments, I encourage them to think about who they are coming from, the explanation of the comments, if comments are repeated by multiple people, if they have questions for the commenters that can be answered, and what their personal goals are for their writing. This thoughtful approach can help you sort through the noise and make productive improvements to your text. No piece of writing comes out perfectly formed on the first try. Not all writing is revised. Take advantage of the opportunities offered to you in the classroom, whether it's through peer workshop, meeting with your professor individually, making use of a writing center, or sharing work with friends and classmates on your own outside of the classroom. Ultimately, the key to growth as a writer is being open to feedback and being willing to consider the opinions informed writers offer you. The goal is to feel confident enough in your ambitions and to adjust your writing accordingly.

Wrapping Up

I hope this chapter has helped introduce you to our topic, class format, and practical considerations that can be applied to considering writing throughout the book. From here on out, each chapter will consider a different topic related to object writing, so we can go more deeply into reflection and exploration. As I mentioned above, please consider referring back to this chapter as you complete the assignments throughout this book.

2 PERSONAL COLLECTIONS AND COLLECTING

What Is Collecting?

My mother always said she understood she could build a business in antiques, because she was married to my father. He was a collector and she saw how the collector's mind worked. She always knew if there was a collector for it, she could earn a living. Collectors are different from those of us who are not. They have a single-mindedness that drives them to either complete, find the best examples, every variation, and/or catalog what is in existence. All one needs to do is take a look at social media to see how collecting manifests in newer generations and the satisfaction people take in what they hunt down. Even casual observers find gratification in seeing something in its entirety, a complete history, all the things. Great museums and institutions were built on personal collections. Ideas from collections and collecting permeate our conception of the world of objects.

What can we learn by looking at what we collect? What do the collections of friends, family, and acquaintances tell us about who they are? Where did we get the idea to collect something, and why does it have value for us? How does public perception affect what we collect, and how we feel about our collections? How much is too much or not enough when it comes to acquiring items?

There is a compulsion for many of us to acquire every example of something that ever existed. We might find examples of this in our own households or on the television shows we watch. This may come in the form of blatant consumerism where the buying of expensive handbags, clothing, or shoes is something to admire and aspire to. Satisfaction may reside with less expensive items that come in many colors and versions, like the Stanley Mugs that have taken over the internet.

Collecting has a long history, and these collections have become the basis of a lot of our most revered cultural institutions, something I will discuss more in depth in Chapter 4 on institutional collecting. While we may not have the purchasing power of a robber baron or new money, we may have a passion for something more attainable given our limited resources in terms of money and time. Even if we are not collectors ourselves, we undoubtedly know someone who is.

In class, I define a collection as something that was intentionally put together by a person, not something that happened as a result or side effect of another action. For instance, we may collect paper bags because we are too lazy to package and recycle them on a regular basis—this is not a collection. If, however, we keep paper bags from stores we like and admire, and go out of our way to purposely acquire them, this could constitute a collection. I have students who collect Apple boxes, and I have students who never throw anything away—there is a difference in how things are acquired and why things are kept when it comes to collecting. These items may or may not have monetary value, but they need to have value in other ways.

This difference of intention will be key to understanding why people feel they need to own more than one of something. These objects may be functional in nature, but more often than not, collections are not used in their entirety due to the sheer number of items included and the limitations of how much we can use at one time. There are reasons for collecting beyond the understood purpose of the individual items.

We must consider the fact that to collect something is to want to possess it and control it. Possessing items is an important part of collecting. Even collections that are given away or set up as museums after a person's death carry a burden of the collector on how they should be shown or displayed. We can think of the lawsuits over the preservation of the Barnes Collection in Philadelphia or the collections of Donald Judd that I will discuss in Chapter 4. Collections may be exhibited in full or hidden away with only a few objects on display, with the rarest items locked up or hidden from regular view. There is something about being able to control the access to and display of these objects because we own them that makes them more special to us.

The chapter will focus on personal collections and collecting. In the following sections, I will look at object fixation and object as inspiration to continue consuming. These examples invite writers to consider personal collections and the collections of other individuals in their lives. In Chapter 4, we will extend the idea of collecting to public institutional collections and collecting. First in this chapter, we will examine why certain objects inspire admiration and even obsession that propels people to keep buying them en masse. This consideration spans casual collecting to the extremes of hoarding and purging. I consider the following ideas in this chapter: what makes an object collectible, the satisfaction of the hunt to complete or create a collection, how we determine what antiques and art objects/collectible objects are valuable, hoarding, purging, minimalism as virtue, collections as status, and collections on social media.

Object Fixation

Object fixation isn't a new concept. All we need to do is look to Donna Tartt's *The Goldfinch* to see how obsession with an object or acquisition of it can shape an entire life, personality, or storyline. Why are we so obsessed with certain items? What does it feel like to look at the unattainable or try to acquire the unattainable ourselves?

Humans love to consume stories about people who go from rags to riches. We especially like stories about someone unearthing objects that change their financial, personal, or professional futures. This trope appears in real life and on the screen. I think of Howard Carter's unearthing of Tutankhamun's tomb in 1922, or in the movies, I think of the fictional Indiana Jones finding the Holy Grail. While these examples are of larger-than-life explorers, there are also many tales of average people finding objects that turn out to be worth thousands on the *Antiques Roadshow*. We may hold onto an idea that collected objects can radically change our lives, no matter how unlikely the scenario is. It is tempting to think—if I just acquire or unearth these magic items, all the challenges in my life will be solved.

We might know people in our lives who feel this way and are always looking for the things that will make them whole (and those things may change). We might spend time making Pinterest boards devoted to singular kinds of objects or visiting institutions that hold particular pieces that capture our imaginations. Items may become emblematic of our bigger desires or dreams.

When I was studying creative writing as an undergraduate student, my teacher Denise Duhamel introduced our class to a collection, featuring her writing, titled *Mondo Barbie.* The volume contained writing on the wide range of reactions individuals had to this most collected of dolls. This book struck a chord with me since my first collection was of Barbie dolls. I started with an inherited vintage accumulation from my aunts, which blossomed into spending my time at garage sales, flea markets, and antique shows hunting out rare outfits and dolls in their original boxes. I got value guides as gifts for holidays and engaged in researching the rarest items and dolls, coveting hard-to-find international pieces from Japan and Europe.

As the editors of *Mondo Barbie* explain about the history of Barbie and what she represents,

> Why Barbie? Because Barbie is the problem. She is an American icon. The product of an adult fantasy of a girl-child's toy. Or is Barbie the adult's toy and the child's fantasy? What happens when the adult fantasy collides with the child's fantasy? Sparks fly. You would have no "Angry Woman" issues of RE/SEARCH without Barbie. This book is the answer to millions of prayers. At last revealed—all that misplace Barbie angst, all that childhood conditioning, torture, and repression. A home for brave Barbie survivors who can finally step forward. "My name is . . . I had a Barbie." (Peabody and Ebersole 1993: 3)

Barbie has been written about ever since she was introduced in 1959. She was too sexy, too disproportionate while also strangely aspirational in terms of career and independence. She represented both the fears of adults and hope in the imaginations of children. I was not a child who had a sophisticated relationship to Barbie. When my colleague Darra Landman told me her Barbies were First Ladies and judges, I felt bad that mine were only preparing to go out on dates and drive sports cars.

Interestingly enough, there has been a recent resurgence in the fervor over Barbie brought on by the namesake movie in 2023. We can see with Barbie the lifecycle of an object that holds public fascination and represents larger ideals. Certain objects, as the editors of *Mondo Barbie* explain above, hold a fascination for their audience that goes beyond the objects themselves. Barbies have come to represent something larger to collectors and audiences, whether it be a sense of history, women's rights, or a passion for fashion.

In his book *The System of Objects*, Jean Baudrillard theorizes not only how we classify and order objects, but also what drives people to value certain items and choose them for collecting. As he describes in his second chapter on collecting,

> Let us grant that our everyday objects are in fact objects of a passion—the passion for private property, emotional investment in which is every bit as intense an investment in the "human" passions. Indeed, the everyday passion for private property is often stronger than all the others, and sometimes even reigns supreme, all other passions being absent. It is a measured, diffuse, regulating passion whose fundamental role in the vital equilibrium of the subject or the group—in the very decision to live—we tend not to gauge very well. Apart from the uses to which we put them at any particular moment, objects in this sense have another aspect which is intimately bound up with the subject: no longer simply material bodies offering a certain resistance, they become mental precincts over which I hold sway, they become things of which I am the meaning, they become my property and my passion. (Baudrillard 1996: 85)

It is no revelation that many of us feel a sense of identity based solely on the objects we collect and possess. Baudrillard begins to explore how objects go beyond even our feelings for other people. Owning a collection of certain items can give the individual power and a sense of belonging or identity. The ability to define ourselves by what we own is significant in our global economy.

Baudrillard continues to define what happens when an object becomes something that is collected and loses its functional or original purpose. In addition, once we have a collection of something, its original purpose for us may change.

> The pure object, devoid of any function or completely abstracted from its use, takes on a strictly subjective status: it becomes part of a collection. It ceases to be a carpet, a table, a compass or a knick-knack and becomes an object in the sense in which a collector will say "a beautiful object" rather than specifying it, for example, as "a beautiful

> statuette". An object no longer specified by its function is defined by the subject, but in the passionate abstractness of possession all objects are equivalent. And just one object no longer suffices: the fulfilment of the project of possession always earns a success or even a complete series of objects. This is why owning absolutely any object is always so satisfying and so disappointing at the same time: a whole series lies behind any single object, and makes it into a source of anxiety. (Baudrillard 1996: 86)

In his terms, collected items can be signifiers of something beyond the self and satisfy a need for fulfillment. However, it is impossible to have everything, because there is always more. This is the conundrum for the collector—there is a satisfaction to the collecting but an emptiness in the collection. For some of these reasons, collectors are often described in theory and literature as deeply problematic. Some speculate that collecting is a way to fill in an emptiness or unmet need through object acquisition and holding. This is why Baudrillard believes there is something always impoverished about the collector (Baudrillard 1996: 86), because there is an endless need that can never be met.

In his famous essay, "Unpacking My Library: A Speech on Collecting," Walter Benjamin gets to the heart of the competing passions that compel a collector. He describes the different urges involved in collecting as he describes going through the boxes of his own book collection. By analyzing his own feelings during this process, he attempts to give insight into what possesses the collector's mind.

> What I am really concerned with is giving you some insight into the relationship between a collector and his possessions, into collecting rather than a collection. If I do this by elaborating on the various ways of acquiring books, this is something entirely arbitrary. This or any other procedure is merely a dam against the spring tide of memories which surges toward any collector as he contemplates his possessions. Every passion borders on the chaotic, but the collector's passion borders on the chaos of memories. More than that: the chance, the fate, which suffuse the past before my eyes are conspicuously present in the accustomed confusion of these books. For what else is this collection but a disorder to which habit has accommodated itself to such an extent that it can appear as order? (Benjamin 1968: 59–60)

For Benjamin, it's not about the type of object but what the process evokes. He muses on how the collector can find a sense of control and order over her own memories through the process of acquisition. Although this semblance of control may be false, it is nonetheless an essential part of collecting. "Thus the life of a collector manifests a dialectical tension between the poles of disorder and order" (Benjamin 1968: 60). We attempt to control life by controlling what we own and how we take care of it.

This feeling is most likely recognizable for anybody who has purposely pursued collecting. How do we feel about owning and acquiring these objects? What stories do we tell others and ourselves about our collections? At what point does collecting stop—when you run out of room, when you've attained as much as possible given your means, or when you've lost interest? What is the endpoint and what is the result of all of the collecting? Benjamin explores what it feels like to finally possess the items we spent so much time pursuing.

> The most profound enchantment for the collector is the locking of individual items within a magic circle in which they are frozen as the final thrill, the thrill of acquisition, passes over them. Everything remembered and thought, everything conscious, becomes the pedestal, the frame, the base, the lock of his property. The period, the region, the craftsmanship, the former ownership—for a true collector, the whole background of an items adds up to a magic encyclopedia whose quintessence is the fate of his object. (Benjamin 1968: 60)

This attempt to freeze time and the memories attached to the item, from the quest for it, to the study of it, keeping and displaying it all coalesce to fuel the passion. So much of the process for Benjamin is not the owning, but the act of collecting the items. This can be related to mementos of travel as we will discuss later in this chapter and to public collections we will examine in Chapter 4. There is a universal interest in controlling our sense of self and of time through the things we collect.

The Thrill of the Hunt

A lot of my students report that upon completing a set of something, they lose complete interest in it. Like Baudrillard and Benjamin in the pieces discussed above, they discover that the stories of acquisition can be just as important as the object itself. For many people, the thrill of collecting is in the hunt. A lot of this has been lost in the age of the internet where, in general, things have become more accessible and searching for items is not as difficult or exciting as it once was. Items that were collectible when I was a child, selling things at the flea market almost instantly lost their value with the rise of early resale sites like eBay.

Changes in technology, which in turn changed the nature of the hunt, may be a big reason we scratch our heads at what older friends and family have collected. Hummels, collector's plates, Lladro, and Beanie Babies come to mind as some previously popular collectibles that have tanked in monetary value and rarity. In fact, these items were marketed to be collectibles with the idea that if you invested in these keepsakes, their value would increase more than money in the bank. What happened was what once seemed rare became readily available once the internet came around. Things that were hard to find became easy to find and abundant in a way that took the monetary value away from the objects themselves and made the search for the items a thing of the past. For many, this also took away the personal value of their collections and left a bitter taste in the mouths of those who spent money and time amassing these objects. Ideas of value constantly change for reasons more complex than this example, which is why we are often curious or confused about what people collect and why.

While the hunt has changed for some, it has only become a more exciting game for others. With the rise of the internet, people can now feed their very particular collecting interests and share them with an audience. This can manifest in examples of tracking down the things they see in vintage TV shows, ads, and movies and sharing them on social media. With the age of good visual search engines, it has become even easier to find these items and keep them as trophies. For instance, finding outfits worn by Carrie Bradshaw on *Sex and the City* has gone viral, inspired by Lauren Garroni and Chelsea Fairless' Instagram and podcast *Every Outfit*.

With new accessible technologies, we get to witness what it's like to be a person like me who goes to thrift stores, auctions, and estate sales to unearth items for resale and collecting. Influencers stream videos on social media where they hunt through shops, dumpsters, and garages, showing the goods they find as they unearth them. What was once a private passion expanded to television shows like *American Pickers* and *Antiques Road Trip* before moving to social media where it has become mass entertainment for those looking to experience the excitement of excavating a treasure. There is something exciting in the idea that you can still find something amazing in the midst of all the chaos if you just apply yourself, and even better, we can now experience it vicariously through these videos.

Although many are fun and interesting, I sometimes find these videos overwhelming and sad. While it can be thrilling and exciting to watch items being found and rescued, there is so much stuff in the world that most of it remains where it is found. The dumpster diving videos especially lay bare the waste created by companies and businesses. So yes, there is joy in the hunt, but there is also sadness. We can see so clearly how value is based on experience, perspective, and audience. While some people hunt for high-end fashion, some look for scrap metal and low-priced children's toys. We hope in the bigger picture that there is a person to find value in all of the things.

In the first few years living in New York City, I spent my time hunting for antiques, something that made me feel in control of my environment while also supplementing my meager income as an assistant professor. Antiquing has always been a safe and engaging outlet for my energy, one that allows me to get outside of my head. I've done this ever since I was born, and since I could drive and live on my own, have done it everywhere I've lived.

Personal Memoir

After presenting at a writing conference, I was solicited by an opinions editor for the New York Times to submit a piece on antiquing. While it was never published (welcome to the rollercoaster that is publishing!), I share a version of it here to show my own experience hunting for objects in Brooklyn, New York.

I'm at it again—ping-ponging around Park Slope on foot, cruising quickly yet purposefully down the streets looking for chalked signs, flyers, tables sticking out from the fronts of brownstones onto the sidewalk, crowds of people—anything that signals there is a garage sale. It's amazing how much ground I can cover, faster than the hunters in cars and on bikes—it is the reason I wear down my shoes so quickly. Empty backpack, a pocketful of cash, a back-up checkbook and I'm off to seek treasure.

I am a third-generation antiquer with a long history. At three days old I am scooted in a banana box to auction by my mother, at five, I'm in corduroys with my thermos hocking Barbie dolls at flea markets with my grandmother. Soon I'm ten years old and working carefully through lots of dolls with my parents at Sotheby's, flash to fifteen and I am doing antique shows carefully pulling Victorian silver out of locked cases. When I'm twenty-three I'm standing in the hot midday sun for hours at estate sales to escape my graduate school writing, and now back in NYC, I am an assistant professor who runs the streets alone. Antiques are something you can never give up.

My friends always know where I am on any given weekend and I am not able, despite my efforts, to convince them to tag along, although they do look forward to the stories of my exploits. There is always a story. I am better on my own, anyway, no one to drag in erratic patterns, second guess my sanity, explain my purchases to—only me to carry my stuff. My boyfriend sits in wonder as I come in and out weekend mornings carrying 50 lb parcels, telling stories of whom I met and what I bought and more importantly how much I spent.

In my neighborhood in Brooklyn I am a familiar antiquer, but not easily pegged. None of the regulars knows who I am or why I do this, but after two years I can recognize them all by face. It is a skill I learn early on, know who your competition is and is not. My parents have known hundreds of people by face, but when I ask their names, they draw a blank. You can know people for years only by the objects in their hands. There is the man who takes something off the table in front of me, bullying the seller until they take eight dollars instead of twelve. The guy who only buys name brands—he must do eBay since everything you sell online has to have a name and buying this kind of stuff is an easy and efficient business. There is the man who gives me his card every time I see him; I have at least ten of his cards in my drawer. It's always the same, "If you ever get an antique, I'm the guy to call." His cards are always slightly bent and dirty, made at home when color printers were the new technology. There are the men who marvel at my "good eye" and tell me so, I giggle; they don't know I have been doing this since birth. The woman is local and the only other female beside myself. She buys jewelry and is quiet but early, always there a little after I arrive. The two men who travel together are more aggressive, they pound on doors, they stand in doorways, they are verbal and angry when the sale doesn't look as advertised. This one is just in from California and deals in records, he recognizes me, "Yeah, I know who you are, you were wearing the same shirt yesterday," whoops.

I hit Craigslist the night before to map the sales—it's important to spot the fakes. Grandma's attic, antique jewelry, porcelain, no address, too early in the morning, too far out, with a Tumblr site full of photos—people throw sales up there to get people off track so if there is something really legitimate out there, they can have a small advantage. Like apartment hunting there are codes and you need to learn how to read them, understand where addresses are, areas that are fruitful. Park Slope is the perfect place for this weekend ritual—a collection of people who have been here since the 70s and are now moving to greener pastures, young newly married couples disposing of expensive useless wedding gifts and the wealthy who are often not too concerned with something's value making room in their basements all create a virtual hotbed for a good find.

The ritual of garage saling starts from my first memories, getting in the car early mornings on Saturdays to follow a carefully constructed route with my grandmother. When I am little, we start planning our garage sales for the weekend from the newspaper on Thursday nights. She has an area map and places she normally chooses based upon past hits and the wealth of the area. It is a classist system—if there was never any money in the town, we don't bother going there because the likelihood of finding anything monetarily valuable is considerably less. We cut out newspaper ads and arrange them carefully on a piece of shirt box cardboard with tape and notations about which looks best, what time they start and who says "No Early Birds." There is an easy dividing line—Grandma gets most things except for dolls but in general, if I spot something, I get to keep it.

This week I dart lightning fast across a block in Gowanus to a large black metal candleholder from a Catholic Church. It's a spectacle with over 60 red tea lights, coin container and a large metal cross in the midst of the rows of brick houses. It's price, $100. "It's my wife's, but I'm sure she'd be willing to bargain," says a middle-aged man with his two children in tow guarding the items for sale.

It turns out this piece has a recent world traveling history, one that extends beyond the fate of poor John Pastor whose "In Memory of" placard sits slightly tarnished on top of the change collector. I test out its rusty wheels and giggle knowing my boyfriend is out of town. I could put it right in the kitchen of our one-bedroom railroad, if only I can make a little room. But I could never wheel it home, so $65 and a friendly delivery later, it is mine, sitting underneath my pot rack.

Something about garage sales gives me superhuman strength both physically and mentally. In a way this is how I have spent weekends all my life and the way I have found best to fill the loneliness. Whether through death, a break-up, boredom, or frustration with work I can retreat into something where I am independent and knowledgeable. Growing up with two generations of antique dealers for family will do that to a person. In fact, antiquing from the time I am born has given me a preternatural confidence, a certainty that no matter what happens in life, I can always entertain myself, even support myself with the antiques and the antiquers, and I can love it.

So, now I wander the streets of Park Slope. Planning my route rather haphazardly the night before from Craigslist, I scour for listings that look promising. The local vultures will hit up certain sales before any other—anything listing jewelry. With the price of scrap metal being so high now, grandma's tiny gold chain or mother's silver set have never commanded so much attention. People are hungry and just like for the prospectors, precious metals lead the way to a full belly. There is always a method to this, cross it off the list or really go for it.

Hoarding

We are all inundated with images of hoarders and hoarding, collecting gone to extremes. We can see this on shows about the pursuit of items like *American Pickers*, where things are usually plucked from barns and homes overflowing with stuff. Popular television shows covering hoarding have been running for years, and the genre has expanded to include multiple franchises. From hoarders to flipping houses, animal hoarding, and millionaire hoarding, the general public can't get enough of these stories. A&E's show *Hoarders* had its start in 2009. I, like many others, was hooked. There is the voyeuristic tendency you can indulge in looking into lives that you would otherwise never know about, much like watching people search for antiques. There is also something about excess and extremes that engages an audience. The sheer amount of stuff in these homes makes the shows captivating.

One of the most notorious or well-documented cases that caught the public's imagination was the history of the Collyer brothers. Living a life hidden away in a shared New York City brownstone after inheriting wealth, their day-to-day lives as well as the nature of their deaths among their stuff intrigue people today. Their case is considered one of the first that led to the classification of hoarding disorder.

In their book *Compulsive Hoarding and the Meaning of Things*, writers Gail Steketee and Randy O. Frost talk about the ubiquity of hoarding and how the disorder has even led to its own language.

> Hoarding is far from rare, and Collyer-like cases appear with regularity, so that references to the Collyer brothers can be found in emergency services and legal arenas. Even now in New York City, firefighters talk about a "Collyer house." In New York City housing law, tenants who fill their apartments with clutter and fail to maintain sanitary conditions are called "Collyer tenants." Collyer tenancy in New York and many other cities across the country has become a significant problem. (Steketee and Frost 2011: 12–13)

There is a seemingly endless supply of hoarding cases to fuel the shows we consume. Since most of us live in a world where stuff exists in abundance, we wonder what the line might be for us. What pushes a person from a collector to a hoarder? How many possessions are too many? How do we decide?

Steketee and Frost discuss the difficulty of defining hoarding and how popular depictions affect our perceptions of over-accumulation and what we should value.

> The boundaries between normal and abnormal blur when it comes to hoarding. We all become attached to our possessions and save things other people wouldn't. So we all share some of the hoarding orientation. The passion of a collector, the procrastination of someone who hasn't take the time to put things away, the sentimentality of one who saves reminders of important personal events—all these are part of the hoarding story. (Steketee and Frost 2011: 14)

The fear of being labeled a hoarder is enough for many people to purge their possessions. It is an idea in the back of the mind that influences our consumption patterns and how we see ourselves. Is it strange to keep what I keep and toss what I toss? We will go more deeply into these ideas in Chapter 5 on what is left behind.

There is a lot more to hoarding disorder; it is a common complex and multilevel disorder and at its core, it is about more than stuff. "Many people with hoarding problems have a predominant theme to their hoarding, such as fear of waste, the allure of opportunity, or the comfort and safety provided by objects" (Steketee and Frost 2011: 15). Objects can be comforting and protective for many of us. I personally love the idea that a hoarder has an ability to see what others don't—value in the otherwise valueless or a possibility in the broken. As an artist, I consistently keep items that I think I can repurpose in future artwork, but I admit this can quickly become a problem, necessitating a regular reevaluation of my materials.

> Although hoarding is considered a mental disorder, it may stem from an extraordinary ability. For hoarders, every object is rich with detail. We disregard the color and hue of a magazine cover as we search for the article inside. But if we paid attention, we might notice the soothing effect of the colors, and the meaning of the object would expand in the process. In this way, the physical world of hoarders is different and much more expansive than the rest of us. Whether we look at them and see limitless potential, limitless information, limitless utility, or limitless waste, the people in this book are undeniably free of the usual rules that affect how we view and treat our stuff. (Steketee and Frost 2011: 15)

It is hard to distinguish what has value to us in the moment and what might have value in the future. This is something I will explore in more detail when I discuss trash and refuse in Chapter 5.

Many writers have explored how socioeconomic factors and changes in manufacturing are more responsible than personal predilections or mental health conditions for our excessive accumulation of things. How can we see something as a personal affliction when society engenders it? According to Bill Brown in his book *A Sense of Things*, mass production in the Industrial Revolution changed our ability to buy cheaply manufactured goods, and this changed our relationship to things.

> One could quite simply declare, after the century turned, that Americans lived in an "age of things." But the effort to sell things, to purchase things, and to accumulate things had an inevitable result: "We realize that we do not possess them; they possess us." The point

> wasn't just that Americans were "stifled with the sense of things," but that they now lived life peculiarly possessed. (Brown 2004: 5)

This mass production seems to have increased and increased as has our appetite for things and spawned entire industries, including my work helping people clear out estates, to help others deal with and organize their stuff.

In many ways, objects have become comfort and a way to replace human interaction. We are inundated with stories of robotic pets and humans meant to keep the elderly safe and mentally healthy. Studies are finding that interactions with AI can be more comforting than talking to another human. Gen Z proudly carries around stuffed animals because they are comforting and they have inspired older generations to indulge their own love for comfort objects. As Brown asks here, how often have you found yourself talking to a thing? What is it about objects that makes us feel both overwhelmed yet safe, and where is the line drawn?

> What desires did objects organize? What fantasies did they provoke? Through what economies were they assigned new value? Through what epistemologies were they assigned meaning? Today, how do we ask material objects to represent us, to comfort and help us, to change us? Today do we collect thing in order to keep the past proximate, to incorporate the past into our daily lives, or in order to make the past distant, to objectify it (as an idea in a thing) in the effort to arrest its spectral power? Today, why do you find yourself talking to things—your car, your computer, your refrigerator? Do you grant agency to inanimate objects because you want to unburden yourself of responsibility? Or because you need to mark how overwhelmed you are by your material environment? Or is it simply because you're lonely? Because, unlike a child, you don't have a toy to talk with? (Brown 2004: 12)

Objects have come to replace what used to be fulfilled through human interaction. In an increasingly isolated world where personal comforts and technologies allow us to separate from others, many find connection in the objects they surround themselves with.

> It nonetheless concerns the slippage between *having* (possessing a particular object) and *being* (the identification of one's self with

> that object). It is a book about the indeterminate ontology where things seem slightly human and humans seem slightly thing-like. In other words, this is a book about humans and things that tracks the metamorphosis of one into the other. (Brown 2004: 13–14)

Separating our own identities from what we surround ourselves with is part of the challenge of object writing. Understanding our own compulsions and values and how they relate to societal influences and opportunities helps us reflect on the complexities of our impulses and where they stem from.

Minimalism

On the opposite end of hoarding would be people's obsession with minimalism and what it signifies. In my classroom, I take students through sets of popular examples to help them understand how a minimalist lifestyle has been turned into an elitist goal. Looking into Kim Kardashian's clean white house or the other visions we are exposed to on various media, we can see how the minimalist lifestyle has been touted as aspirational. This may seem in opposition to many of the ideas we have gone over in this chapter, which focus on accumulation, but the core ideas within minimalism make its tenets quite similar. The idea of collecting versus accumulating is a lot about choice and control. On both ends, we examine how we choose to spend our time and money, what results from those choices, and what it can signify to ourselves and to others.

I ask students—what would it mean to be able to choose all of the objects that surround you in your life? This is not a luxury many have. From the things we need to function to the things we acquire to live, we come about these objects in a variety of ways, not all intentionally and with purpose.

For instance, we might have hand-me-downs from relatives, inherited objects, things that do the trick that we bought because they were on sale, gifts from family and friends, items we purchased at random in different states of mind, what we can afford, what fits in the space we have, items that are easily movable if we don't have steady housing, what is required for work, school, or living, and the objects we choose because we like them. The idea that we would be able to carefully curate every object in our lives is a fantasy for almost everyone. That we would have unlimited space and resources to spread out and time to curate our items is unrealistic. That the only things in our lives are things we carefully choose and purchase bears no resemblance to reality. It would cost a fortune in time and money to have only the things we want in the way we want them.

Minimalism or having less is often touted as a more sustainable and responsible option. As we can see from the exploration above, that is not always the case in that to achieve a minimalist aesthetic one might be required to purchase more things to change, organize, contain, or hide what we have. Sure, there is value in having only the things we need, but determining and acquiring only exactly what we need is not always that straightforward and easy.

An approachable and mainstream idea of minimalism comes from Marie Kondo and her KonMari method, which was popularized mostly through her 2014 book *The Life-Changing Magic of Tidying Up: The Japanese Art of Decluttering and Organizing*. Kondo creates a set of rules to make cleaning and organizing accessible, to rid oneself of what doesn't "spark joy," and to use her methods to keep things clean and tidy. Of course, ironically, the success of her book led Kondo to create a series of products that one can buy at the Container Store. Having less or showing less clutter leads to more things to buy. After having children, Kondo remarked how her methods were less useful. We see again the setting up of an ideal and the falling back to a reality of the messiness of life.

Television shows, like Netflix's *Swedish Death Cleaning*, provide a joyful take on a dark topic. In the show, three experts help individuals who are close to the end of life choose what to keep to represent the past and future, what to let go, and ease the burden of stuff for themselves and for their family members. Each of these people is facing the reality of a future they will not be present for, and the concept is to celebrate that we are all mortal and that the possession of things will not change that fact. This is a conscious uncoupling from our stuff for an improved life and legacy. It shows the power objects have to overpower our real joys in life and how letting go for a simpler existence with less stuff can be freeing for everyone.

There are competing ideas here. If our lives are clean and empty, they are controlled. Yet, the acquisition and display of stuff, no matter in what amount, is what allows us to express who we are. Minimalism, more than most models, may require us to consume and collect new sets of items to live up to an ideal. Personally, I have always been more of the opinion that I would never trust anybody with a tidy desk, a quote often attributed to Albert Einstein. We can learn a lot from considering the push and pull of collecting and refining our possessions and what these actions say about us to others.

Assignments and Student Examples

Assignment #2 (Informal "Low Stakes") – Collecting

For this week, you need to interact with a person who has a collection. This can be someone you know or don't know. You then need to write about your interaction with this collection and explore what this collection inspires in you. This collection needs to be something accessible to you in real time as you will need to experience the collection firsthand and post a photo of the collection to this board. Your writing should be one to two pages double-spaced, closer to the 2 mark. You will be sharing these pieces with the rest of the class and I will share the photos next class.

Intention of the Assignment

This assignment requires us to now move beyond our own personal stuff and into the stuff of another person. It is a Low Stakes opportunity to take a close look at a friend or an acquaintance who has a passion for something. It is often used as an opportunity to take a look at the collections of a family member. For our purposes, it doesn't matter if we know the person or not; both options have value.

For those of us who are not collectors ourselves, this is an opportunity for us to begin to assess why someone might collect something and what it means to them. It also allows us to write through our feelings about seeing something and understanding why someone has personally collected the items.

We might not immediately know someone with a collection, and that is okay. The purpose of this assignment is to research to understand a personal connection to collecting and what compels a person to pursue it as a hobby or passion.

Student Example Assignment #2—Collecting

Amy Diop—Books

Books are something almost every household contains. Especially if you are in a family home books may line the walls, all gathered by parents, kids, grandparents, and others. Books are something we all arguably collect, but a collection that lacks intention. So I wonder if the collection lacks intention if it's even a collection. I have been lucky to have spent some time in the spaces of book collectors with intentions. When the pandemic started I went into an immediate panic. At the time I was still living in Manhattan in a one-bedroom apartment. The thought of being quarantined in a small apartment alone because my mom was an essential worker terrified me. I am a very social person and being completely in solus often takes me to really dark places. I was getting older and already having many issues with my childhood home. My partner offered me a solution to my fears and invited me to stay with them and their family in their six-bedroom house with a backyard in Brooklyn. Although I had many reasons to be opposed to it, I knew ultimately that it would be better for me just spatially, there would be a safe outdoor space, more privacy, and human interaction to help keep me afloat during this questionable time.

I had lots of worries about living with another family, and my levels of comfort were being challenged for many reasons. I had the utmost free time ever because we were in a pandemic and I was on a gap semester, so I was not attending online classes. I seemingly was a restless body in the house since everyone else had work to do. I was at a very transitional point in my life and spent most of my time in my head or trying to escape it. It was doing me very little good. My partner's mother Florence is a very different maternal figure than my mother. She is a very busy and detached woman because of her intense job and has a very foreign love language to me. It was getting to me living so closely with people I was really struggling to build a connection with for many socio-economic reasons as well as others. One day I got out of the shower and went into my bedroom and there was a stack of fashion books on the bed. There were great texts and editions that allowed me to dig deeper into Prada, Schiaparelli, men's dress, Carine Roitfeld, and so many quintessential fashion influencers. I was confused about who left all these books for me because they were so on the nose in my interests and taste, I thought maybe it was my partner but also it was very out of their behavior. Later when everyone finished their work and we sat for dinner, Florence asked me if I did any reading today. I then understood she had left all those books for me. It touched me so much because I instantly understood this is her way of showing care and interest in me; she really had just been observing me these first couple of weeks and made me feel so seen and understood by leaving these books for me. The next morning, she invited me downstairs to her section of the house and showed me her highly organized collection of books on fashion, politics, culture, art, etc. Her collection of books instantly made me admire her, and feel closer to her. All of a sudden in my eyes she became a true renaissance woman. She is incredibly well-traveled due to her career but the way she absorbs the things she experiences is with honor, not self-obsession, which is something I think many people lack nowadays.

Florence's collection of books is something I still return to now even though I no longer live in her family home. Organized by date and topic, her collection makes it so easy to take books in and out like a personally curated library. So often there has been a book I wanted to purchase but could not afford or even find anymore, and sure enough, Florence has had it.

Whenever I find myself idle-bodied in their home now I almost always go to her bookshelf and look for new texts to throw myself down a new rabbit hole. Her collection truly made me respect her and see her, the same way her offering of a bite of her collection made me feel seen. As I have gotten older I do not really have anger towards privileged people the way I did when I was a bit angstier, but it all comes back to what people with privilege do with it. Florence's collection, I feel, is her way of taking her privileged experiences into a tangible shareable value for someone else. I personally admire others willing to share but in a way that will benefit the person that you are sharing with and is not a self-inflated moment of look what I have and you do not.

Essay #1 (Formal/High Stakes Assignment) – Collections

For your first formal piece of creative nonfiction writing, I want you to continue considering the idea of collections and collecting. For your first week of class, you investigated an object from your bedroom, what story it told about you, and what it might mean to others. For this past week, you looked at the collection of another person, their reason for collecting, what a collection means, and how it might be viewed by people outside of the collection.

For our first large piece of writing, you will continue investigating the idea of collections and what we personally collect and why. You can think of things you have collected yourself or that others have collected, but your exploration should be rooted in objects that are real and material. You may consider the extremes of collecting like hoarding and purging, maximalism and minimalism, cluttercore, intentional collections or unintentional collections. The most important thing is that the collection (however you define it) tells a story, perhaps about family, relationships, values, culture, or any of the themes the readings have that imbue the collections with complex meaning.

Consider what the authors you have been reading for class have been doing.. How can this help you write your own piece? Think about your peers' pieces and comments; what strikes you about their relationship to objects?

The essay should be about four to six pages, double-spaced in its final form. I encourage you to get this first draft as close to completion for our next class where we will do a formal peer review. You will also receive written feedback from me for revision. This piece will have multiple versions, so really go for it! The more you get on the page the more we can work with it!

Intention of the Assignment

For this first formal essay, students take a deeper view of collections and collecting, informed by the readings and theories we have discussed as a class. Some of my favorite pieces have come from this formal writing assignment. The topic might help you connect to a parent or a person you admire that has a true passion for things. In this way, it might help you to look at what you collect yourself and why.

We can get frustrated, not immediately seeing ourselves and others as collectors. But most people, when they look closely enough, find they have even a small curated collection of items that they seek and value. For some, it might be makeup or fashion; for others, it might be tea cups or stickers; and still others might find their passion for manga and books comes through.

This essay leads to complex discussions and considerations of why we devote time, money, space, and energy to purposely pursuing or keeping collected objects in our spaces.

Student Example Essay #1—Collections

Jools Dembo—Satin Shoes

I am 12 years old, in a room that I'm in would be peculiar to anyone not familiar.

One wall is lined entirely with mirrors and horizontal wooden poles are drilled into the walls. There are 13 girls, including myself, all in identical uniforms of the same black Capezio leotard. Our hair is pulled back in a tight bun complete with dozens of bobby pins that poke our scalps in the most painful places.

We spend the next two hours volunteering our bodies to excruciating pain. Our legs quiver as we hold Degagés. We grit our teeth as our teacher presses her foot down onto our backs to ensure that our hips are fully on the ground as we hold middle splits against the wall. Our toes bleed within 10 minutes of pointe work and it's not uncommon for someone to twist their ankle and then get right back up, ignoring the pain. We dance through broken toes, shin splints, and torn Achilles tendons and we are trained to make it look easy.

If you ask a ballerina how they feel about ballet, the answer will most likely be that they hate it. I hated it too, but it was my passion. The best way to describe a dancer's relationship to the sport is as a toxic romance. My middle school years were spent leaving school early to make it to ballet on time. I spent every day from 3:00 to 9:00 at the studio, trying to finish up essays for school in our ten minute breaks. My weekends were spent off at dance competitions with cringe worthy names like "Star Power" and "NRG" or at 7 hour long auditions for ballet summer programs.

Ballet is a structured art. Every single movement must be perfect. If your leg is even one degree above where George Balanchine declared it should be in his choreography, you were wrong. Yet the studio was my safe space. The intense structure was a welcoming distraction to a world that felt so out of control. There, in the world of precise movements and instruction, I could let go.

Many small children are enrolled in ballet class but as I got older, the numbers dwindled. My close friends at school who had been in beginner ballet with me didn't care about dance by the time we were 8. They didn't understand why I couldn't hang out after school or on the weekends. They didn't get why I couldn't skip dance, just this once.

The age of 11 is a critical moment for a ballerina. For many, it is when they are allowed to go on pointe for the first time. It is what so many of us dreamed about for years, as we watched the older girls at the studio performing variations from *Coppélia* and *Swan Lake*. It is when we all must decide which path to take: Is this a hobby or is this a career?

I never doubted that ballet would be my career. In my fifth grade yearbook, I am quoted as saying that, "In 20 years, I will be dancing with the Royal Ballet in London." I counted down the days until I could go on pointe and the day that it happened will always be one of my happiest memories.

My dance teacher at the time, Miss Kathy, took a group of us to buy our shoes with our parents. I was the youngest in the group, feeling proud that I was the only 11-year-old that year with feet that had been deemed as "strong enough" to endure the pain of pointe.

I must have tried on at least ten pairs. *How will I know if they're right?* I wondered. I didn't want the shoes if they were too comfortable. There is a reason that when the Russian ballerina Anna Pavlova set out to create a more comfortable pointe shoe that many dancers resented the idea. The pain was a rite of passage. In the dimly lit store, I spent hours cycling through Griskos, Blochs, and Suffolks before eventually deciding on a pair of Russian Pointes.

I bought a new pair of pointe shoes every other week, thanking my parents over and over for spending the $100 every time. I remember when my teacher first declared that my shoes were "dead" and that I needed a new pair by class next week. Pride bloomed within me. I was a real ballerina.

There was something within me that couldn't bear to throw out the worn down structure of cardboard and fabric. I fantasized about doing an interview with *Pointe Magazine* in the future and talking about how I still had my very first pair of pointe shoes.

After I kept that first pair, I found that I couldn't get rid of the second, or the third, or the fourth. The shoes tell my story with ballet. How the Russian Pointes that I bought the first time had been discontinued by the time I needed a new pair. Or the time that I tried out Grishkos, only to despise them and kill them within two days of dancing. In the shoes I see my teacher telling me to invest in a pair with a stronger shank, since my arches were pronounced. I see when I made the switch to Bloch Sonatas, the shoe that would become my favorite.

While doing a closet cleanout over winter break, my mother asked me if I wanted to get rid of the shoes. I can only imagine the look on my face was filled with horror and worry. The shoes may have no physical use anymore, but they still mean more to me than most of the things that I own. I can't picture a world where I don't have those shoes in my possession, even if their only use is collecting dust in a closet.

Whenever I look at them, I feel a twinge of sadness. Also residing in this box is a brand new pair of pointe shoes. No ribbons or elastics are sewn in them and the shank isn't even cut up with scissors (a practice that became crucial to my process of breaking in my shoes). I bought this pair right before I quit ballet.

I stopped dancing when I was 15. That year, I had worked my way into my studio's Junior Company, the elite competition team for my age group. When I arrived for my first day at our summer bootcamp, something felt off. I pushed through my feelings for the first few days, trying to focus on the hundreds of crunches that the outsourced choreographers were requiring of us. But I just couldn't shake the feeling that something was wrong.

I left gradually, first deciding that I would only take classes with the company and not attend competitions. This would also allow me to take an extra ballet class, the style that was my true passion over lyrical and jazz. I performed in *Cinderella* in the fall, spending every waking moment outside of class drilling my variation into my bones. But it began to feel like a chore.

In January, I sat down and had a tear-filled talk with my ballet teacher, Miss Georgia. I told her that I was done. I just couldn't keep doing it anymore. I wish that there was a precise reason I could pinpoint as to why I felt this way. Maybe it was that I grew up and realized that no matter how much talent I had, my body type and height would always hold me back from a professional career.

Growing up dedicating your entire life to something and then stopping is a specially isolating feeling. Ballet was my entire world. Every waking minute was spent in the studio. My favorite movie was *Center Stage*, my favorite show was **Dance Academy**, and my favorite book was *A Very*

Young Dancer. I wore my hair in a bun to school as if to signal to my peers that ballet was who I was, not just something that I did.

Leaving ballet is a unique experience that only other "retired" ballerinas can understand. I still find myself doing Tendus while I brush my teeth or absentmindedly marking the variation that I performed in Cinderella. There's a slight sting when I see a ballet or walk by Lincoln Center now. I know that the dream that I put countless hours into will never come true. But ballet will always be a part of me and I'm forever thankful to the younger version of myself who decided to keep those pale pink, satin shoes.

3 AUTOETHNOGRAPHY AND RESEARCH

What Is Autoethnography?

How do we extend our personal understanding of objects into the larger cultural conversation about what society values? How can we explain our experience through the lens of a larger world beyond the self?

Any good writer of creative nonfiction knows that to fully understand the self, you have to be willing to research the self in order to understand how we became who we are. Memory, as we discussed in previous chapters, is fallible, and the truth is based on a contract we establish with readers; that we will do the best we can to be consistent and accurate given what information we have access to. Part of deepening self-reflection is pushing ourselves to understand what outside influences helped inform our personal opinions. Engaging in qualitative research and autoethnographic inquiry can help us extend and expand our own understanding of our points of view to consider larger cultural influences on our valuation of objects.

To start us off, I will use the same explanation I developed in my first book, *Teaching Autoethnography: Personal Writing in the Classroom*, to establish the scope of autoethnography for our work on object writing.

> Autoethnography is treated as personal writing in which the subjectivity of the writer is highlighted and experiences are understood through narrative exploration and storytelling, incorporating other voices, observation, participation, and larger cultural ideas. Using autoethnography in this way allows students to employ first-person research and analyze their own subjectivity in narrative form. The primary focus is on the value of storytelling and examining the self in relation to experience. The approach values the audience and considers the value of analyzing, reflecting on and narratively communicating personal experience. (Tombro 2016: 8–9)

As you can see, we have already looked at some of these concepts in Chapter 2. Now we will work on how to use qualitative inquiry to understand the influence of our surroundings on our perception of objects.

Personal writing has been historically undervalued, yet personal experience is the way that most of us relate to and come to understand the world around us. Starting with personal reflection as we have done so far in this book allows us to more easily come to know how our points of view and provides a basis for growth in understanding how these perceptions were formed.

In her preface to *Handbook of Autoethnography*, Carolyn Ellis gives the best description to date of what doing autoethnographic work can accomplish for writers and researchers.

> For most of us, autoethnography is not simply a way of knowing about the world; it has become a way of being in the world, one that requires living consciously, emotionally, and reflexively. It asks that we not only examine our lives but also consider how and why we think, act, and feel as we do. Autoethnography requires that we observe ourselves observing, that we interrogate what we think and believe, and that we challenge our own assumptions, asking over and over if we have penetrated as many layers of our own defenses, fears, and insecurities as our project requires. It asks that we rethink and revise our lives, making conscious decisions about who and how we want to be. And in the process, it seeks a story that is hopeful, where authors ultimately write themselves as survivors of the story they are living. (Ellis 2013: 10)

Here Ellis, known as one of the earliest practitioners and teachers of autoethnography, focuses on the way intentional personal research connects us to our larger world and surroundings. Diving deeply into our personal connections to the world around us allows us to more deeply understand the significance of our lives. All personal writing is not necessarily autoethnographic, and the book's editors help the reader to understand the difference.

> While all personal writing could be considered examinations of culture, not all personal writing is autoethnographic; there are additional characteristics that distinguish autoethnography from other

> kinds of personal work. These include (1) *purposefully commenting on/critiquing of culture and cultural practices*, (2) making *contributions to existing research*, (3) *embracing vulnerability with purpose*, and (4) *creating a reciprocal relationship with audiences in order to compel a response.* (Adams, Holman Jones and Ellis 2013: 22)

As we push into topics that include cultural influence as well as curation of public objects, we start to augment our self-reflection with larger conversations with the systems that put our ideas into place.

In their book *Autoethnography*, authors Tony E. Adams, Stacy Holman Jones, and Carolyn Ellis give a summary of what autoethnographic stories provide to the readers. "The stories we discuss in this book—autoethnographic stories—are stories of/about the self told through the lens of culture. Autoethnographic stories are artistic and analytic demonstrations of how we come to know, name, and interpret personal and cultural experience" (Adams, Holman Jones, and Ellis 2001: 1). In other words, personal writing and research on individuals and their experiences can help us understand the larger world around us as well as ourselves as part of a larger framework that influences our points of view.

The qualitative inquiry practices we use for creative nonfiction object writing may include deep real-time observation, interviewing family and friends, visiting cultural institutions, and looking into the history of our objects all while considering what personal experiences have informed our perspectives on their value. While not all writing you do with objects will be classified as autoethnographic, these concepts can be applied to help you as a writer understand how to expand the scope of your work.

This is definitely not a theoretical book on material culture or how an object acts as a way to research past histories. For our purposes, this can be overly scholarly, inaccessible, and somewhat dry, missing the personal and individualized elements so prized by the creative nonfiction writer. I cannot give a history of qualitative inquiry in this book either. Instead, our idea here as writers is to pursue lived research to add meaning to our experiences and use larger reflective practices to understand the personal lens through which we view our things.

In the first set of assignments in Chapters 1 and 2, the focus is on the personal and our relationships to family and friends. In this chapter, we keep focusing on the personal by first asking writers to think about individual objects that have personal value to them and what the stories are that we tell ourselves about them. We will consider how we deepen our observational practices to add complexity to our writing. We then extend our inquiry into considering our larger surroundings and beliefs.

Autoethnographic analysis helps writers consider how we define and relate to mementos, nostalgia, family history, relationships, and cultural ties communicated through objects. These objects may be common objects and uncommon objects, easily categorizable or utterly unique. While this chapter will focus on how autoethnographic inquiry relates to personal nonfiction object writing practice and reflection, this inquiry process will also be applied to publicly collected objects. Institutional collections will be introduced in this chapter, but covered more in depth in Chapter 4. Much like Chapter 2, you can apply the pedagogical ideas in the section to all assignments in the book, especially those that follow in Chapters 4 and 5. In this chapter, I use the lens of gender for our assignment to ask writers to consider how they view an object versus how their larger cultural surroundings code that same object for consumption.

Researching the Self

As we explored in the previous chapters, objects we keep don't necessarily have monetary value. There can be many reasons to hold onto something or to pursue collecting it. In the first exercise for class, students were asked to look to their own bedrooms for an item they kept close and investigate what that object means to them.

Keepsakes may be something we cherish because of how they make us feel. One of the most popular sets of sentimental keepsakes that my students keep when they go off to college is groups of cards from family and friends. A close second is pieces of jewelry from an older relative, romantic partner, or friend that reminds them of their bonds to that person. Items such as these can become even more important to us when we are entering new environments for the first time. They can connect us to family and friends who are no longer present in our daily lives and can remind us of where we came from. As we move into more High Stakes writing assignments, assignments with multi-step revision, we are looking to take initial impulses and make them more meaningful. Understanding what forms our relationships to these objects beyond this self is what adds depth and layers to the writing. Taking something like a keepsake and looking into the family history of the item can be one way to dip our toe into autoethnographic practices.

A wonderful example we consider in class examines the history of a small object that was owned by an author's mother. In "The Silver Pin," Susan Rubin Suleiman discusses a pin she inherited from her mother, one that is featured in a photograph she has of her before the family emigrated from Hungary to New York City. Past the moment caught on film, Suleiman never saw her mother wear the brooch. She wonders,

> So why didn't she wear it? Was this modest relic of postwar Budapest unworthy in her eyes? (I think my father bought it for her shortly before the photography session, as a sign of prosperity and survival). Or was it perhaps associated with a country, and a city, that she had no desire to remember? She has lost most of her family in 1944, deported with the help of the Hungarian government—she never spoke about those uncles and aunts and cousins, and I have no memories. (Suleiman 2007: 188)

Her mother didn't reminisce about Budapest and worried about her family and daughter assimilating in their new home. The brooch, when brought to a jeweler, had no monetary value, so the author is left to understand its value alongside the complex history of what it represents about her mother and her family's history. Why her mother chose to wear it, the history and changes it represented, and what it means to keep and reflect the larger cultural associations that accompany a simple item.

Researching the self may seem like a bizarre idea and one that doesn't make immediate sense. Our memories are our own and we may feel a strong sense that we know who we are and where these moments fall in our personal histories. However, new associations and understanding of our personal histories can emerge from personal and family research. Like in the story of Suleiman's pin, this can mean talking to people about your memories, looking at documents, photos, videos, emails, posts, texts, anything that can help you to understand how your memory or interpretation of an item might be different from the other histories of perceptions of that item.

This is an especially important skill when we discuss distant memories. We grow and change through time, so it is only natural that our version or understanding of past events might grow and change with us. Are you representing the point of view of your current self or your past self? How do the facts line up with the memory? How does getting other perspectives help us to better understand our own?

In our classroom, looking at cultural systems and attitudes helps us come to understand how much our valuing of possessions is influenced by the worlds we inhabit. While there is a large international population at my institution, even if we all grow up in the same country, we would have different ideas of objects based on a large number of factors including where we grew up, who our family was, our relationship with family, ideas about religion, our socioeconomic status, our exposure to ideas outside of our immediate surroundings, as well as myriad other factors.

It is important to introduce the fact that we are shaped in large part by circumstances outside of our control into our writing practices. To ignore that fact is to misunderstand what informs our ideas and our writing. This is the key to active reflection—beginning to break down what factors influence our points of view and come to understand how and why those influences are important to us and our connection with others.

A lot of times as writers, we are encouraged to separate the self from our writing when autoethnographic practices encourage just the opposite—to lean into the examination of what motivates and informs our points of view.

> The crisis of representation also motivated researchers to acknowledge how their own identities, lives, beliefs, feelings, and relationships influenced their approach to research and their reporting of "findings." This focus on representation encouraged qualitative researchers to search for more transparent, reflexive, and creative ways to do and share their research. Rather than deny or separate the researcher from the research and the personal from the relational, culture, and political, qualitative researchers embraced methods that *recognized* and *used* personal-cultural entanglements. After all, as researchers we are interested in exploring and understanding the experiences that have salience in our lives, whether these experiences thrill, surprise, intrigue, sadden, or enrage us. (Adams, Holman Jones, and Ellis 2001: 22)

We should be excited to have the opportunity to embrace our pasts and current circumstances in order to understand why we feel the way we do about the things surrounding us.

Active Observation and Interviewing for Writing

There are techniques we can employ that will help us gain the perspective we need to extend our reflective capacity. These techniques ask us to place the self in spaces and to interact with people in order to write about them. Actively engaging in unfamiliar environments and with new people for the purposes of writing may be a new idea for many writers. As mentioned in Chapter 1, we are used to harvesting our memories to develop subjects for our writing. Especially in classrooms, assignments might require us to reflect on the past, be it immediate or distant. This is normal as starting with what is familiar can be a way of coming to understand ourselves as storytellers and is a good stepping stone to deeper reflective writing. From there, we need to push ourselves to do observational research to gain new perspectives and additional information about our subjects.

Real-time observation, often called embedded observation, is not only a practice in autoethnographic inquiry, it also has a long history in the field of creative nonfiction, where writing is not only meant to entertain but inform the reader. In "The Five Rs of Creative Nonfiction," author Lee Gutkind, by many considered the godfather of creative nonfiction, breaks down his approach to teaching creative nonfiction research methods. He models his methods by situating the reader within a narrative of his time in operating rooms, showing and then telling how they can follow his tips for embedded research. He encourages students to experience the world around them to gain perspective to avoid the "egocentrism" (Gutkind 1996) inherent in personal writing. Researching a world outside of what we already know provides us with both perspective and information that will engage the reader. Paying close attention to details and talking with members of a community can be key to connecting with a larger understanding of a world that is less familiar to us.

While we start with the known in my class, I consistently ask students to actively engage with their current surroundings for the purposes of writing. This is why for the very first assignment on bedroom objects (Assignment #1), I ask students to choose something from their current space rather than a past space they inhabited. What is the difference? By observing the present for writing purposes, we can begin to find new ways to capture and explore detail, especially the five senses. When we observe for writing, we have a wealth of information at our fingertips since we are collecting it in real time. Making oneself aware of surroundings in an active way can be challenging in that we often tune out the white noise of the spaces we pass through and inhabit out of necessity. By not remaining in the past, we are forced to consider where we currently are in life and how that affects the way we interact with the world and its objects.

Thoughtful observation is the opposite of tunnel vision—it is letting in all of the environmental information so we can consider what informs our understanding of our spaces. Many of the assignments throughout this book require writers to enter new spaces or observe ordinary spaces for the purposes of writing. In the following chapter, writers are asked to visit a local institution in order to write about it, and in the final chapter, writers are asked to examine the trash in their environments. Like the bedroom exercise, we can learn a lot about what is important by simply paying attention.

I encourage you to hone in on the people and things surrounding you and to use the devices you have on hand to record impressions of experiences as you have them. It is best to write about a trip, for instance, close to the time you take the trip. Since we lose a lot of the evocative details the further away an experience is, note-taking can help us capture the feeling of being somewhere in real time. We can collect more information than we may have access to when discussing a distant memory. I take notes on my phone since it is usually what is on hand, but writers can write in a notebook, take short videos, pictures, or even record the sounds of their surroundings to provide themselves with data for their writing.

As part of observation, we also want to interact with others who have important relationships with the objects we are writing about. In my book *Teaching Autoethnography: Personal Writing in the Classroom*, I give instructions for formal interviews for the purposes of research writing. While those guidelines could also be helpful here, the nature of research for object writing is a bit different. We are looking to have organic conversations with those who interact with and value objects. For our purposes, there are central goals we should have when talking to others:

> The purpose of the interview is to help you gain insight into the perspective of another member of your subculture. This can be valuable on a number of levels and for a number of reasons. It can help you understand the subculture more as an outsider, offer additional

information you can use to examine your own positionality, and provide interesting narrative content for the final project. (Tombro 2016: 70)

From these interactions, we are trying to create relationships with others in order to deepen our understanding of our relationships to the objects we are discussing.

For the previous assignment on collecting (Assignment #2), students will often do a somewhat informal interview with the person who possesses the collection. This is the first time they step outside of their own experience and enter the world of somebody else. They will have conversations around why they started their collections, what they enjoy most about them, and why. It is important that these conversations allow room for the subject to share their own stories and not feel like they are responding to a number of canned questions. I encourage students to reach out to people in their lives that they know value something enough to collect it and then visit with that person to share the experience of looking at the collection and talking about it together. My students find it valuable for them to engage in the experience authentically and find a connection that is not over-considered.

While discussing experiences and topics with family, friends, and subjects is always helpful for our writing, interviewing becomes more relevant for the writer as we discuss institutional objects. In Chapter 4, I will discuss how talking to curators and archivists can open up our understanding of how things are valued outside of our personal experiences.

Gendered Objects—Extending the Narrative Outside of the Self

As we move deeper into researching the personal and transitioning into public collections, I ask students to consider how cultural standpoints on gender can affect the way we view things and what cultural markers say to us about objects. I will use gender here to more clearly demonstrate autoethnographic inquiry and its applications.

Points of view on a complicated topic such as gender can have to do with exposure and access as well as attitudes and social mores related to concepts and things. This is intimately related to my work as the creator and coordinator for Women and Gender Studies at my home institution. Gender is just one lens that you can employ to extend the view from interior to exterior influences on how we view objects. Other topics can be employed to achieve the same goal depending on the topics you cover in class or your own personal writing. As I mentioned in my introduction, my work in the field of Women and Gender Studies influences the examples I use in my courses.

In her Object Lessons piece for *The Atlantic*, "The Still Misunderstood Shape of the Clitoris," Naomi Russo talks about how an open source 3-D model of the clitoris, developed by French researcher Odile Fillod in 2016, has changed the understanding of this complex organ not just for the general public but also for medical professionals. I bring in an example of this 3-D model to pass around for show and tell during class. While my students are used to seeing visual examples of the phallus in art and visual media, most have never seen, let alone interacted with, a representation of the clitoris. This show and tell is a vivid and memorable way for students to understand that we become accustomed to viewing the genitalia of roughly half the population as something understandable and knowable while half the population is rarely represented.

Social factors and lack of knowledge contribute to misinformation about the clitoris. This model was created to help open the conversation and dispel misinformation. "At 10 centimeters in length, from the tip of the glans to the end of one 'crus' (or leg), the model clitoris is bigger than expected. That's tactical: It was created to dispel misinformation. Many dictionaries and even medical texts dub the clitoris as 'pea-sized'" (Russo 2017). While it cannot completely alter the narrative, Russo explores how physical objects help our understanding of the world and putting representations out there can change more than our perception; it can impact our health and our rights. My students are often amazed to see the inexpensive plastic model and for the first time see a representation of this part of the anatomy. I bring in something unexpected to show the larger assumptions we carry around, and an object can truly alter our perception of reality.

In the book *Queer Objects* edited by Chris Brickell and Judith Collard, we extend our discussions of gender to include what objects can represent in terms of sexuality and lives lived and how the lens we use to view these objects can change our understanding of their meaning. "Queer lives include a range of objects: the things with which we fill our houses, the gifts we share with our friends, the commodities we consume, the things we wear and the technologies we use to communicate with one another. But what makes an object queer" (Brickell and Collard 2019: 11)? This book gives photographs and stories of special and mundane objects that take on alternative meaning based upon how they are situated in people's lives.

> By exploring this wide range of things and places, arranged a little like a cabinet of curiosities in a sequence of rough themes—identity, growing up, literature, sex, art, domesticity, memorialization, regulation, adornment, activism and leisure—*Queer Objects* reveals both the diversity of social classifications and human experiences and the continuities in the world of love, sex, friendship and intimacy. (Brickell and Collard 2019: 21)

How do the lenses we use and the context we have change our understanding of things? Here I will give examples from two of the chapters contained in the book and how they help us begin to understand the role of gender in objects.

During a trip to Portland and a visit to Powell's books years ago, I had come across *The Cunt Coloring Book* while browsing the Women's Studies section. Having been familiar with Betty Dodson's vulva sketches and paintings, I was amazed I had never heard of this text and quickly bought it. Inside, like any other coloring book, were images to be filled in with color. The difference here was that there was a range of line-drawn vulvas as the subjects. In *Queer Objects*, there is a piece on Tee A. Corinne's *The Cunt Coloring Book* by Margo Hobbs who explains:

> The book offered its audience a queer viewing experience by refusing to conform to heteronormative conventions of looking. Theories of the gaze articulated in the decade following publication established what Corinne already knew: existing images of women's bodies and genitals neither satisfied her sensual desires nor reflected the way she, as a lesbian, saw women. The available mass market images invoked patriarchal codes that mastered the female body by exercising an objectifying and consuming gaze. Corinne's book eschewed hierarchies and established intimacy between viewer and image: the viewer's tactile senses were engaged by looking. (Hobbs 2019: 121)

Queerness, in a lot of ways, is about being subversive. It has always been a subversive thing to represent bodies unmitigated, and by looking at this through a lesbian lens, Corinne was able to present a different view of the bodies she drew that invited an alternative form of viewing and consumption. This book is contemporaneous with other artistic output which involved vulvic representations, such as Judy Chicago's *The Dinner Party*, and thus is part of a larger public conversation which developed in the 1960s and 1970s about women's rights and their place in the art world.

In *Bloomers and Monocles*, Nikki Sullivan and Craig Middleton similarly look at articles of clothing and how their adaptation by early lesbians changed them as signifiers. This is an example of how objects that were already in existence for one gender or purpose came to be coded in a completely different way because of who wore and possessed them. "This chapter focuses on two objects from the Migration Museum in Adelaide, South Australia: a nineteenth-century meersham pipe that features the carved figure of Amelia Bloomer, and a monocle that dates from the first half of the twentieth century" (Sullivan and Middleton 2019: 327). In this exploration, Sullivan and Middleton explore how trousers and monocles were adopted by counterculture women and lesbians to signify a shared set of values for life and living.

The body and how we dress it has always been a part of gender identity. Beyond this, the body itself has been coopted for commercial reasons in order to sell and market ideas and objects to the public. While I have complicated feelings about Margaret Atwood's attitudes toward feminism, her piece for the *Michigan Quarterly Review* is a favorite in my classes. In "The Female Body," Atwood lists ways women's bodies have been used as objects and manipulated in shape by other objects. One of the few pieces of fiction I use in my teaching, I like it for its list-like qualities that put so many examples back to back that they become hard to ignore. We sometimes spend up to an hour just discussing what each of the items listed is and its function in gendered femininity. Her list of items meant to modify the body to different tastes includes garments and adornments that are both familiar and of another era.

> The basic Female Body comes with the following accessories: garter belt, panti-girdle, crinoline, camisole, bustle, brassiere, stomacher, chemise, virgin zone, spike heels, nose ring, veil, kid gloves, fishnet

> stockings, fichu, bandeau, Merry Widow, weepers, chokers, barrettes, bangles, beads, lorgnette, feather boa, basic black, compact, Lycra stretch one-piece with modesty panel, designed peignoir, flannel nightie, lace teddy, bed, head. (Atwood 1990: 491)

This substantial list of how the female body has been used in marketing hits home for a lot of my students, who study business communications and design. Atwood goes on to talk about the turning of the body into objects of consumption.

> The Female Body has many uses. It's been used as a door knocker, a bottle opener, as a clock with a ticking belly, as something to hold up lampshades, as a nutcracker, just squeeze the brass legs together and out comes your nut. It bears torches, lifts victorious wreaths, grows copper wings and raises aloft a ring of neon stars; whole buildings rest on its marble heads.
>
> It sells cars, beers, shaving lotion, cigarettes, hard liquor; it sells diet plans and diamonds, and desire in tiny crystal bottles. Is this the face that launched a thousand products? You bet it is, but don't get any funny big ideas, honey, that smile is a dime a dozen. (Atwood 1990: 491–2)

Each of us can recognize objects from these lists that are part of our own households or experiences. They may be objects that have made us roll our eyes or that introduced us to how others sexualize bodies. They may be familiar and represent how we treat our own bodies or consume media and internalize the reality of what is possible. They are funny and serious, frustrating and dangerous all at the same time.

We might have experienced being categorized in particular ways based on how we dress and what we own. It is not uncommon, for instance, for my students to discuss how they may not feel comfortable having objects they like surrounding them or wearing what they prefer because of the ideas about gender people project onto them. Conversely, they may feel the need to own certain things to signify their gender identity to their communities as well as the larger world. Grappling with what the objects we own signify about our beliefs on gender is a topic covered by Roxane Gay in her book, *Bad Feminist*. In her last chapter, she explores all the ways she considers herself a bad feminist and how this complexity within herself is what allows her to take a complex look at how ideas about gender and belief inform how she operates in the world.

> I love dresses. For years I pretended I hated them, but I don't. Maxi dresses are one of the finest clothing items to become popular in recent memory. I have opinions on maxi dresses! I shave my legs! Again, this mortifies me. If I take issue with the unrealistic standards of beauty women and held to, I shouldn't have a fondness for fashion and smooth calves, right? (Gay 2014: 315)

Gay admits to suppressing parts of herself and at times being uncomfortable with her own likes and needs. She wants to be seen in certain ways, but she also wants to be true to herself. These contradictions make her a narrator we can come to trust because we can identify our own levels of confusion through her honest, detailed reflections.

I ask students to use deep observation and informal interviews to take a look at gender in their own lives to start to connect their personal lived experience with cultural expectations. We are bombarded with stereotypical, nostalgic, and sometimes problematic depictions of gender across the board. What does this mean? And how does it affect how we view things in large and subtle ways? What aspects of representation do we embrace or reject in our own lives and what we own? These considerations lead to larger complex conversations about why people persist in using bodies and representations in particular ways.

Beyond the considerations of our own cultural and generational experiences of gender and its constructs, we begin to think more broadly about why certain ideas take hold, especially ideas that would be considered problematic by most people today. Why do people continue to collect and purchase objects that are offensive at best and dangerous at worst? Why do we cling tightly to tradition and nostalgia as ways to justify an unwillingness or inability to change? How does this change how we view ourselves and what we own?

I ask students in my classroom how they would feel knowing me if they found out I had a personal collection of offensive objects that represented women, even if I explained that it was because I was studying them. They immediately look at me askance because they know it would change the way they viewed me, even if I had a good explanation or academic justification for the collection. I assure them they will find no such collections in my office, but it is important for us to consider the power of representation in objects and how it can change how we view the world and the people who buy and hold these objects.

In the following assignments, we will see how the techniques discussed here are applied by students through assignments on gendered objects.

Assignment and Student Example

Assignment #4 (Informal "Low Stakes")—Gendered Objects

This week we are thinking about gender and objects. What makes an object gendered? Personal, cultural, and societal associations can make people associate gender with objects. The owning of certain objects can be seen as scandalous, wrong, and/or unacceptable based on gender connotations. On the flip side, we can feel certain objects are symbols of gender affirmation and are even necessary to own, display, or wear to express gender identity. Objects can be claimed and reclaimed as symbols of gender freedom or used as examples to upend binary categories. Colors, uses, smells, and even shapes of items can associate them with particular groups of people.

Pick a gendered item to write about. This can be something you own or something that someone else owns. Its creation doesn't need to have been intentionally gendered. What makes this object gendered? What do you think of its categorization? Does its gender association carry meaning for you? For society? Your writing should be one to two pages double-spaced, closer to the 2 mark. You will be sharing these pieces with the rest of the class, and I will share the photos next class.

Intention of the Assignment

I use this writing as a way to start to consider how objects are coded and how this coding can affect the way we perceive the things in our lives and even determine our relationship to them.

Many students involved in advertising, marketing, and product design majors are attuned to how to create campaigns and objects for an audience. They are used to considering the finest details and focusing on minutiae in how objects are designed. What they might not have focused on as much is how they are already participating as an audience for these created objects and how everything from color to shape to sounds and smell can make a difference. Using these observational skills to examine their immediate surroundings can yield many surprises.

I like to bring in mass-market menstrual products as an example for this exercise. We talk about the nature of these objects—the plastic is made to not make a sound because there is shame embedded in the need and use of these objects. They are almost always summery colors with light blues and pinks and purples. They are made to be discreet, thin, narrow, collapsible, small, and inconspicuous. I ask, what feelings arise as we pass them around the room? Is there discomfort because these are supposed to be private objects to take care of something normal but not publicly discussed? Do they have scents, what are they? Watermelon? Is it normal to want to have your genitalia smell like a Jolly Rancher or a cool breeze (whatever that means)?

They are then asked to think creatively and observe things that currently surround them that they find to be gender coded. This is an interesting exercise and can be a little difficult, which is part of the fun. The object doesn't need to have been created with the intention of appealing to certain gender identities; the goal here is to see what is implied in its creation, presentation, and ownership. I will be talking more about archival collections in the following chapter. This writing exercise is a way to cap off their initial exploration of qualitative inquiry methods, how society influences our perceptions of objects, and how our personal histories and experiences shape our understanding. This work will lead us into the next step of grappling with public collections and the cultural implications of personal stories.

Student Example Assignment #4—Gendered Objects

Renée Dery—The Bra

Right now, I only own one bra. It's a cheap black triangle bra from H&M, a fast fashion purchase that I'm not proud of but a secondhand bra just really isn't my thing. I purchased this bra right before I started my freshman year at FIT, with the intention of wearing it as a shirt. At this point in my life, I was vehemently anti-bra. I had just come out as a lesbian, and I was emerging out of the pandemic aiming never to shackle myself with a bra ever again. This was of course a point of contention between me and my parents, but my boobs were small enough to the point where it honestly didn't make much of a difference. So, I threw out the two Victoria's Secret bras I'd had since the 8th grade (the only bras I'd ever had) and officially freed the nipple. However, two years later I'm back to wearing my little black bra most days, which definitely would come as a disappointment to old me, but I'm glad I went through that phase.

I was very upset about puberty when it finally started hitting me in the 8th grade. I didn't like the fact that the support systems I had in place had to be updated, mostly because I didn't know how to fix them. My first ever "bras" came sewn into the interior of white tank tops. These tank tops were given to me in elementary school as training bras, just like the rest of my friends. But as they all started to develop quicker than me and move on to fancy bras with cups and sizes and hooks, I stayed deeply attached to my tank tops. I didn't end up taking the trip to the Victoria's secret to get fitted until the tail end of the 8th grade, and by that point I had probably needed one for a year and a half. I stayed deeply self-conscious about whether or not my classmates could see through to my white tank for the entirety of middle school by choice. If I had asked my mom for one, she would have gotten me one, but I couldn't admit to myself that I was actually experiencing puberty. I wanted to stay behind.

I eventually adapted to the fact that I had grown into a teenager, and learned how to deal with all the troubles that came with it. That included wearing my nude underwire bra every day, and putting on makeup and straightening my hair and only dressing up when I knew that my friends also were. And then there was the pandemic. And then I was a lesbian. And all of a sudden, all of the pressure I felt to conform to the idea of a perfect teenage girl was reversed. It was replaced with the urge to differentiate myself, to separate myself from all of my classmates that had made me feel so insecure my whole life. So, I dyed my hair bright green and ditched the bras, and it worked. I had a new persona, everyone thought that I was cool now, not just the weird girl who doesn't talk in class. As I went off to college, I stayed true to my no bra promise for a while. But at a place like FIT that is not something that separates you from the crowd. Here, all the originality I had just made me fit in. This came with a pretty dramatic loss of personhood, and I felt myself scrambling to figure out who I am amongst a crowd of people who were just like me.

It's been two years since then, and I don't want to say that I've figured it out, but I think I've made many strides. A major change and my own apartment certainly helped, but the gender aspect of it all is still quite blurry. If I don't wear a bra, I get self-conscious about the fact that I've developed into a woman, just like in middle school. I habitually put on a bra now, as I did in high school (absolutely no underwire though). Occasionally I don't wear a bra, and I can still understand how freeing and wonderful the experience can be. In one way, it reminds me of my womanhood, because of its gendered nature. However, it also helps to suppress my chest, hopefully drawing less attention to my womanhood.

This is one of those things that doesn't have a proper resolution. I don't know how I feel about bras, because we have a complicated history, but I do think that I feel better when wearing one. To me, they mark stages in my growing up as a girl, and as of right now I'm accepting my black triangle bra as another stage. And I'm sure I'll find out soon what the next stage is going to be.

4 PUBLIC OBJECTS AND COLLECTIONS

Institutions and Collecting

What is it worth preserving for the future? What are we willing to do to make sure that it will remain intact for the public? We briefly touched on the concept of value in Chapter 2 on collecting. There is a saying in the antiques business that just because something is old doesn't mean it has value. In fact, this is a point of contention for a lot of people who do resale, especially those who help people liquidate and clean out estates. Most value is family history or sentimental value, and most items have little of that value to the relatives of that person at all. These realisms can raise a lot of emotions in people, and the final blow can be to learn that usually a lifetime's worth of accumulation also has little monetary value. While this can be a complicated personal issue to manage, as we will discuss more in Chapter 5, it becomes interesting to consider why institutions and businesses spend money, space, and time preserving things for the public and how we can think about that for our own writing. What can objects collected by others and preserved for the public inspire us to write? Who decides what is collected, and how does that affect the way we value the things around us?

Wrapping our heads around what might constitute a public object and collection is always a bit more challenging than looking to the personal. It asks us to consider the places that wield large amounts of money or cultural influence that in turn impact what we see as valuable. Since institutions are run by people, we also need to understand the human factors that determine how decisions about public collections are made.

We may take a lot of public institutions for granted and what they collect as being by default valuable. When we enter a museum, for instance, we understand that we are entering a space that by definition holds things of value. This idea of value can be communicated to us in myriad ways from witnessing the resources devoted to creating and maintaining collections, the fact that we are usually not invited to directly touch the items, to considering the fees we pay to enter these spaces. Similarly, we may assign value to the books in a library because they are collected and maintained, even though we are allowed to access most of these items for personal use. We also often assume value with artworks in public and business spaces, assuming there is always a reason something is displayed or protected in these ways. If an institution is willing to spend copious amounts of money, devote tons of space, create ideal conditions, store, advertise, solicit donations, employ people, do research, and make exhibitions, this lets us know these items have value, whether it be monetary, historical, cultural, or a combination of the three.

In my class, we have interesting conversations about seeing public collections that truly inspired and impressed us and others that left us wondering why they were so special. While we are somewhat inadvertently trained to think things are valuable because they are collected and displayed by organizations, we always confirm that there are many publicly collected items that we don't find much value in.

I often use the example of visiting the town of Marfa with my spouse as a time when I questioned what is valuable about public collections. While it was a great trip with a lot of great art, we were amazed at how Donald Judd had bought and filled almost the entire town with stuff. You could visit multiple dwellings, studios, and offices which were filled with his things, some of it art but most of it an assortment of items he had purchased and kept. From what we were told, his instructions upon his death were to leave the items as he had them displayed in his lifetime. On the tours, our docents described the basements and buildings filled with the items he hoarded, not collected. Most of what was on display beyond his personal artwork was not special; it was just owned and organized by Judd. What is the value in leaving things the same forever, and what does that mean in terms of how we see and value things? If everything is special, nothing is special. That it was collected by an artist makes it special in this case.

In *Stuff: Compulsive Hoarding and the Meaning of Things*, the authors explore how an object touched by someone is deemed more important by most people than a similar object that was not touched by a famous person (Steketee and Frost 2011: 44). "One study, for example, found that children judged an object that had been touched by the queen of England to be more important than an identical object that had not been touched by her. The first object contained an essence not apparent from its physical characteristics" (Steketee and Frost 2011: 45). We can see this idea at work not only in public collections, but in Chapter 5 with inherited items. Why does something change meaning just because it was owned by a particular person and how does that affect how we view it?

Beyond personal connection, we confer value onto certain items based on many other factors—historical value, monetary value, and artistic value being just a few. How we come to this valuation and who makes the valuation can affect how we view it. In the examples above, there are curators, librarians, wills, families, and corporate employees making decisions that affect what we see and how we see it.

What we devote to preserving and displaying a collection can say a lot about who values it and why. It can also indicate who the collection is intended for by how easily accessible it is to the public or to specialized audiences. When we enter the Metropolitan Museum of Art in New York City, we know the things inside are valuable, but why? Perhaps it is because of how the objects are displayed, the building they are in, and/or the fact that we can't touch them. When we see the items at the New York Public Library pulled from the archives and displayed in glass boxes, we know the contents are important. When the Tiffany & Co. flagship store puts on an exhibition, what does it tell us about the value of the things and the brand?

In this chapter, we will be looking at archives and public collections and what they say about cultural values when it comes to objects. We will explore basic ideas behind institutional collections and archives and discuss how creative writers use archives for research and inspiration. We will consider why we enjoy the institutions and public collections we do, from museums to businesses to archives, how storytelling and cultural value influence our feelings of value and appreciation, and how we can access the collections of local institutions to inform our own writing. We will discuss researching collections for creative inspiration, institutional collecting, institutional storytelling, personal value versus cultural value, whose objects are seen as valuable and why, and how public collections help us determine personal value. We will begin by considering archives and museums before we move to how brands use public collections to add value to their objects. I cannot offer a comprehensive history of any of these topics. There is a long history of museum studies, archive studies, and brand development. This chapter is meant to give examples and ways to help you write about and navigate the public collections important to your own writing.

Archives

The most important part of public collections for my students is archival ones. Archives allow interaction with archivists and direct access to items that museums and businesses do not. For the most part, visitors to an archive are encouraged to physically interact with the items. There may be special conditions for this handling, but most archives have public access among their missions because materiality is important for learning. Since archives occupy the biggest part of the work on public institutions in my classroom, I will spend the most time discussing archival collections in this chapter and what we can gain from interacting with them.

At my home institution, students have the opportunity to look at college archives that contain the history of students and structures on our campus as well as view a large collection of mostly fashion-related ephemera, from the Battle of Versailles to historical documents and collections detailing the work of designers. Our collections are mostly used by our design students as well as visitors from the outside doing historical designs and research for television, movies, podcasts, and books. It makes sense that my college would want to preserve and understand its own institutional history and provide resources related to fashion industries because of our mission as a college. Our newly renovated state-of-the-art space also demonstrates that our college values the preservation of these items.

This school archive has significance for my students since they attend the college and have a wide array of interests related to the objects collected by the college. I have worked for the past few years with archivist Karen Trivette who built up the collections and the facility into what it is today. Students typically visit the archives during our class period, and we spend about an hour talking to Karen about her work as an archivist for the college. Students are then invited to examine a series of objects pulled from the collection to use as inspiration for their personal writing. This visit is a way for them to get to know a part of the institution that they may have never seen while also learning what it means to access materials from and interact with them for writing purposes. We get to see what our institution collects, how it demonstrates its core values, and what these items in turn mean to us. Having the opportunity to interact with an archivist like Karen shows them the very human element that forms and preserves collections like ours.

Many colleges use institutional archives as teaching tools for the students. At the University of Illinois Urbana-Champaign, I was involved in teaching a course for the then newly introduced Ethnography of the University Initiative. The goal was to get first-year students to use the university archives in productive ways in their coursework. This access allows students to understand the complex history of the university and encourages them to do qualitative research for writing purposes. By also keeping some of this research in a digital archive, they create a history of this work for others.

Many of us have never visited archives on our own and may be wondering what the purpose of archives is. Almost all of the institutions we are discussing in this chapter have archives, some accessible to the public and some not. Tiffany & Co. has an archive that is not accessible to the public, while our home institutions or local libraries may have collections that are open to anyone for research or inspiration.

I focus on local institutions in my community in New York City that have a varied history, cultural mission, purpose, and way of interacting with the public. By finding different partners that you would like to work with, writers can come to understand the different ways we are taught to engage in these collections and the effect access to them, as well as their exhibitions, can have on us as outsiders. By interacting directly with archivists, we can learn about the work that is involved in creating and maintaining the objects in these collections.

In *Archives Powers: Memory, Accountability, and Social Justice*, Randall C. Jimerson, an archivist and historian, sets up the scope of the function of an archive and those who build it so we can understand the mechanics of public-facing institutions.

> These include: determining what documentary materials will be chosen and protected in the archives; evaluating or appraising the significance of these archival sources; ensuring their preservation from decay, neglect, media instability, and theft; organizing and describing the materials in order to make them accessible for future

> use; providing access and reference assistance; promoting knowledge or archival holdings through outreach and public programs; and conducting advocacy on behalf of archives and archival interests. (Jimerson 2009: xiv)

As we can see from this overview, the tasks for an archive are multi-layered. It is not only to collect objects, but to protect, organize, acquire, and make them accessible to the public in useful ways. Jimerson goes on to discuss how archives work in tandem with other public-facing institutions for the purpose of looking toward the past to consider the future.

> Above all archivists are concerned with the record—its purposes, origins, uses, and values. Their knowledge of records enables them to interpret these records, assist others in using them as evidence, preserve and organize them for use, protect their reliability and authenticity, and ensure their accessibility as either legal or administrative evidence or as conveyers and communicators of culture and human experience. In common with libraries, museums, and other cultural institutions, archives help us to know the past, to understand the present, and to prepare for the future. Although less well known than their information profession counterparts, archivists serve a vital function in society. (Jimerson 2009: xiv–xv)

As explained here, this work may be more hidden than the work of our museums, libraries, and businesses, but archiving serves an important purpose in preserving things for study that also inform these other more public-facing institutions.

Sometimes, we can see the archives themselves visually represented in a more public way. I bring students to the New York Public Library Stephen A. Schwarzman Building to take a look at the now permanent Polonsky Exhibition of the New York Public Library's Treasures collection. These are physical items and ephemera on rotation from the NYPL archives. While some items are always on display, such as Charles Dickens' desk, other pieces are displayed in groupings throughout the exhibition hall. I have students come visit the exhibition each semester so they can talk to a research librarian as well as an archivist to understand what goes into choosing items for this exhibit and what it means to now have this permanent display free and open to the public. I have worked with Ian Fowler and Mia Bruner for the past few years to create a curriculum where students get a guided tour of the exhibition, see some objects from the archives up close, and have the opportunity to ask questions about finding objects for their own research, the larger NYPL collections and how to use them.

At the Polonsky Exhibition, there is a large range of objects on display: NYC maps, the original Winnie the Pooh stuffed animals, early activist texts, toys, costumes, illuminated manuscripts, and much more. It shows a small sampling of the over fifty-six million items held by the NYPL for study. There are many benefits to a trip like this—many of my students have never been to the NYPL at all and do not even know they are eligible for library cards to access collections for their research. The library helps them sign up for one if they don't already have one and learn how to research the collections online and in person. Much like our visits to special collections, students get to talk to an archivist who participates in curating the exhibitions, which allows for a connection between object and person. These objects often form the cornerstones of their formal Essay #2 on Institutional Collections; they are easily visited for free and represent a broad spectrum of what is collected in archives. The way the archival objects are situated, described, and displayed brings up many emotions for those viewing them and helps the students to question their own ideas about value in preservation and curation.

Beyond my home institution's collections and those of the NYPL, I have had the pleasure to work with both the Lesbian Herstory Archives as well as the Barnard Zine Library through my work on my Women and Gender Studies research. Both collections are groundbreaking in their nature because of the unconventional ways they were started and the unique ways they continue to operate and influence others. What they have in common is their open access, which allows the public to benefit from their holdings.

In The Archival Turn in Feminism: Outrage in Order, Kate Eichhorn presents a brilliant overview of the history of feminist archives, using both of these archives among her examples. What is most wonderful about this book is how it values the differences in the collections and how alternative perspectives on the purpose of an archive and how we archive and preserve objects positively influence those who utilize the spaces.

> I ask what might be gained from considering the place of archives and archiving in contemporary feminist activism and knowledge

> production. I specifically maintain that drawing our attention to the archival turn in contemporary feminism is one way to move beyond the generational debates that have stifled feminist activism and scholarship since the 1990s. (Eichorn 2014: 31–2)

Her careful analysis of feminist archives reveals both the radical methods employed by their creators and archivists and how different collections can strengthen our understanding of feminist movements.

The open space of the Lesbian Herstory Archives, housed in a Park Slope, Brooklyn brownstone where a volunteer consistently lives, is a warm and inviting environment that encourages participation in the processes of archiving and interacting with its holdings.

> From its inception, the LHA has juggled various and eclectic goals. Beyond collecting the documents and artifacts of individual lesbians and lesbian organizations, the LHA is "a force for community building among lesbians, providing a welcome, and often a meal or lodging for visitors from out of town and actively networking among lesbians nationally." Although the LHA is the largest and undoubtedly most important lesbian feminist collection in North America, if not the world, and hosts professional researchers on a regular basis (or as regularly as the archive's highly irregular hours of operation permit), its structure and mandate have changed little since its inception in 1974. Over the course of its long history, it has continued to combine private and public spaces. It is an archive with more than one sofa, a kitchen open to volunteers and visitors, and to this day a member of the collective lives in the house, albeit now in a separate apartment on the top floor. (Eichorn 2014: 48)

I have had the pleasure of working with Deborah Edel at LHA to help catalog donations. LHA offers training to people who want to catalog parts of its vast collection, which is housed in a space that is free and open for the public. In my time there cataloging lesbian fiction, I had the pleasure of reading hundreds of pages of material, some published, some not, from donors who chronicled their experiences in earlier decades, creating works that both connected them to others and also captured the feelings of being a queer person when it was less acceptable and safe to exist. Students are welcome to work at the archive themselves and interact with any of their holdings for their own research.

While the Barnard Zine Library is housed on Columbia's campus, its influence has spread far and wide. Jenna Freedman started the Barnard Zine Library and her cataloging methods have made the presence of zines significant in WorldCat and search catalogs far beyond the reach of the physical campus. Freedman has made an inviting section of the larger library where visitors can sit at a large table and pull zines from the shelves to peruse and read. It is a welcoming space that, like LHA, encourages interaction with the materials.

> From the onset, then, Freedman's project has been about collecting and preserving zines for use by Barnard College students, faculty, and visiting researchers and more ambitiously about rendering visible zines and, more specifically, the unique content of feminist zines within library catalogs well beyond the catalog connected to the local collection. To this extent, Freedman's initial proposal and ongoing project has targeted two interconnected sites of activism—the actual space of the library (and in this case, a connected archive) and the more conceptual space of the library catalog and its extended virtual networks. (Eichorn 2014: 129)

I have been bringing students to work with Freedman and her staff for years. Students are invited to freely interact in an open space with original copies of zines that have inspired and created movements within feminism. One of the most notable collections here is the Riot Grrrl collection. Many of my students are familiar with this movement from the 1990s and are excited to get to hold and peruse the actual zines that inspired so much music and girl power. Students from my other courses, who sometimes create their own zines, have been invited to submit their zines to be part of the permanent collection. In this way, Freedman ensures the growth of the collection and the intention to accurately reflect generational shifts and perspectives. It is exciting to get to hold a piece of history that you find empowering and relevant to your own life.

There is a wide range of archives that you can choose to visit and interact with. You can see a broad spectrum of collections in New York City represented here. While most of us don't live in major cities, that doesn't mean there aren't a wide range of places that archive collections. As mentioned, schools, libraries, and museums, no matter what size, are a great place to start. Archives are also available digitally, but since this is a course on materiality, I encourage you to find archives that allow in-person access as well. In fact, many items become digitized only because individuals request that they be pulled for their own research and study. Most archives do not have the money, time, and human power to make everything accessible online. For this reason, it's doubly important to interact with your local archives. Requesting an item to view will put the object in the archivists' hands, something that doesn't always happen with large collections, and also signal that there is public interest in that object or series of objects. Your visit may give the archivists a way to digitize what is pulled and make the objects accessible for many people outside of your communities who would not otherwise have access to them.

As you consider the collections available to you, browse what they have, talk with an archivist or librarian, and through some organic exploration feel out what items inspire you to write. What do you connect with? Whether it be the history of your towns and institutions or archives that contain important pieces of history that you find inspiring, interacting with local archivists always yields new ideas and inspirations for writing.

Museums

A visit to the museum for many of us was the first way we were introduced to the fact that there were things beyond our daily reality that had a lot of value. It may have been a local home or county museum in the communities where we grew up or it could've been a larger trip with school or family to a location known for its collections. It's no surprise that in New York City we have a huge array of museums which contain everything from fossils to historical artifacts and fine art. In this course, we spend quite a bit of time talking about the great museums of New York City, most of them free for students and residents to visit.

In this section I will focus on art museums for my primary examples. The reason for this is that more than other museums, art museums engender particular concepts of monetary and intellectual value through exhibition and curation that more hands-on museums on different subjects do not. They reinforce hierarchies, typically provide less context and less accessibility to the objects they collect. Unlike archives, the public is not invited to interact with the items. Instead, visitors are positioned to view and admire what is on display from a distance. In this way, art museums help us to understand another perspective on how we are taught to value curated objects.

When I talk about a place like the Metropolitan Museum of Art with my students, many of whom are fine art and design majors, my students overall express a sense of detachment. They are sometimes asked to go see an exhibit as part of a class assignment or field trip, but in general, they express a disinterest in the collections found there. From our conversations, this seems to stem from a lack of context for understanding what they are supposed to get from these objects.

I have been discussing my students' general disconnect from museums quite a lot with my colleagues recently. Why is it that so many students don't feel welcome in these museums? When I was a child growing up in New Jersey, it was always a special treat to drive in to visit the Metropolitan Museum of Art. My parents would go directly into the parking garage below the museum, and we would enter through the underground back entrance. I was so enchanted by the exhibits I saw there as a child that I eagerly talked to my grade school teachers about them and tried to recreate Monet's bridges for a third grade art project. Many of my classmates and teachers had visited The Met, and discussing the exhibits there always sparked conversations in class.

Not growing up going to physical collections or having access to them, not taking in media that appreciates or values public collections, plus going into museums that don't provide a whole lot of context for their permanent collections but instead rely on institutional reputation, can make people feel disconnected. It is generally acknowledged in a number of studies that the average person spends less than 30 seconds looking at a piece of art, sometimes significantly less. This is a perfect reason to analyze these connections we have all the more. How do we feel when we enter an "important" museum to look at "important" art? What speaks to us and why? What leaves us cold and uninterested? What museums and exhibits have stuck with you? What exhibitions intrigue you and which are ones you want to skip?

In the many volumes on museum studies and curation, scholars discuss the impacts of context and the human touch that determines what is valued and displayed. In their introduction to the anthology, *Thinking About Exhibitions*, Reesa Greenberg, Bruce W. Ferguson, and Sandy Nairne don't hesitate to tackle the complex nature of museums, diving into critique in their first paragraph.

> With art exhibitions and anthologies, objects and texts are always assembled and arranged according to an arbitrary schema intended to construct and convey meaning. In their mega forms—the blockbuster, the retrospective: collections of complete works or compilations which inaugurate or consolidate a discipline—they lay claim to being exhaustive when they are always incomplete (and often only exhausting). Exhibitions and anthologies are, by definition, selective and exclusive due to the biases of the organizers and the actual or perceived constraints of space, finance, and availability of works. (Greenberg, Ferguson and Nairne 1996: 1)

Here we can see a concise overview of the inherent contradictions found in museums as the authors reflect on how this reality can also apply to their own book. While museums may give the impression of authority and comprehensiveness, they are still subject to the same set of circumstances used to value any item. In these cases, there is simply a larger infrastructure and platform reinforcing the hierarchies. We can see concepts here that have come to play in all of our chapters from thinking about collections to what we decide to throw away. Although a museum may value certain items, this valuation is not necessarily conferred to an audience in a real way. We may understand the signaling of value, but in our personal realities, we may not see the relevance of the items we are asked to admire.

Many books consider how biases have come into play in museum settings and how this can affect our connection to what is displayed. In *Curatorial Activism: Towards an Ethics of Curating*, Maura Reilly explains how her book critiques the bias inherent in the history of art museums, what they value and how they exhibit it.

> My aim as a scholar and curator is to *ferret out*—to tally, to count, and to throw inequities into high relief, laying bare the powerful ideological mechanisms that ensure some artists are celebrated while others are marginalized. I have dedicated the past twenty-five years of my career to attempting to ensure that the under- or un-represented, the silenced, and the "doubly colonized"—those subjected by both empire and patriarchy, for example—are no longer ignored. (Reilly 2018: 21)

Throughout her book, Reilly examines the responsibility of individual curators and other players in the art world in perpetuating systems of value that leave many underrepresented and undervalued. We can start to see the lenses of the museums we visit as we keep these considerations in mind. Instead of considering these spaces neutral, for both good and complicated, we can start to see the culture, history, money, and people who influence exhibits and how things are situated for our viewing.

When I first visited the Walker Art Center in Minneapolis, I was stunned by the number of women artists displayed on the walls of the museum. This shouldn't have been notable, but as Reilly points out, the majority of art displayed in major museums is by white men. "I take as my operative assumption the fact that the art 'system'—its history, institutions, market, press, and so on—is hegemonic, that it privileges white male creativity to the exclusion of all Others" (Reilly 2018: 21). This is not an assumption on Reilly's part as much as it is a fact for most major collections. As a person who grew up loving art museums, I took for granted that the art displayed on the walls was the most important and most worthy of being revered. It never occurred to me that there were multiple systems at play that conferred value on some artists more than others. At the Walker, I felt excited and proud to see all of the art by women, many of whom were not recognizable to me, and how beautiful and inspirational their work was for me as an artist. It made me consider what else I had been missing out on and why.

We can start to consider who funds museums, what original collections and people inspired them, read the mission statements of different institutions, and most importantly take note of what the things within these spaces represent to us. Beyond the awe I had at The Met when I was a child, my favorite museums tend to be smaller and more focused on narrative. Although enjoying his work in major collections, I only developed a real love for the work of Joan Miró after visiting the Fundación Joan Miró in Barcelona. For me, the curators did such an excellent job combining the personal and professional evolution of the artist that it increased my appreciation for his work and contributions to art.

Hopefully, there are museums that you have access to that inspire reflection and connection to what is on display. The sense of awe that can come from viewing a wonderful exhibition or a beautiful item can provide great inspiration for writing. For many of us, our first introduction to writing about museum objects comes from the poetry we are asked to read in school. "Ode on a Grecian Urn" by John Keats is probably one of the most well-known examples of ekphrastic poetry, or writing about an art object.

In *The Gazer's Spirit: Poems Speaking to Silent Works of Art*, John Hollander considers how, "poetry has dealt with in the past, and continues to confront today, particular works of art" (Hollander 1995: 4). Through forty-eight examples he explores the meaning of this written form and how it interacts with art objects.

> Particularly in the nineteenth and twentieth centuries there is a good deal of such poetry, addressing a wide range of good and bad, great and obscure, unglossed or overinterpreted works of art, and taking up a range of stances toward their objects. These include addressing the image, making it speak, speaking of it interpretively, mediating upon the moment of viewing it, and so forth. . . . But they obviously share the common rhetorical predicament of representing in language what is itself representing visually yet something else. (Holllander 1995: 4)

There is something magical about translating a sensory experience into the written word. Hollander, through his consideration of ekphrastic poetry, demonstrates both how the written word augments our understanding of an object and the subject's relationship to it, while also demonstrating the limitations of prioritizing one sense over another.

There are many authors that use the experience of museums and what they contain as inspiration for writing. Most recently, Patrick Bringley published *All the Beauty in the World: The Metropolitan Museum of Art and Me*, which chronicles his decade there working as a museum guard while also looking at the art and interacting with the patrons. In *Lost Wax*, Jericho Parms shares a collection of essays written "largely within the galleries of the Metropolitan Museum of Art." In the essay from which the title is taken, Parms explores the Greek and Roman sculpture court as she reminisces about her own romantic relationships and the relationships of her parents and a couple she meets when traveling.

> Why, when I walk through room after room of Greek and Roman antiquities, do I think of the exquisite and the peculiar, of love? Because these sculptures are allegories preserved. A buxom statue of a woman bears no limbs. A chiseled torso is cracked and headless. Even Aphrodite is missing the arms that once shielded her heroic nudity,

> and beneath the curve of her hips, beneath her ripe symmetrical ass, it appears as if the flesh of her things has been gouged away. These classical forms, created to uphold perfection, have inherited the imperfection of life itself. Maybe I can breathe a little easier now, knowing that the weight of the deities does not sit so squarely on our shoulders—at least not wholly intact. (Parms 2016: 118)

In her essay, Parms is able to translate her own feelings about love and its imperfections through the bodies of the ancient statuary. We can see here how objects in museums can help us find solace for our current feelings through witnessing stories of the past.

Museums, especially art museums, are complicated spaces with multiple levels of bureaucracy that determine what they display and how they display it. In your own communities, explore what interests and inspires you and why. Consider favorite objects and exhibitions you have attended. Consider how the display of the objects invites you to interact with or distances you from them. Reflect on what you value when you enter these spaces and how that can inform your writing about the objects inside.

Brands and Businesses

In recent years, it has become more popular for large and small brands to collect their own items and display them in their flagship locations and/or to maintain archives in support of the history of the brand. They draw on a lot of the curatorial and archival practices to place their companies on the same level as not-for-profit institutions. This allows them to not only act as a retailer but also as an institution contributing to a historical record which in turn adds importance to their reputation as well as adding to their financial power in the marketplace. This can affect the way the viewer and consumer engage with the brand and also how we understand the importance of the items in their collection.

How this trend has been developing in fashion has been discussed quite often at my home institution, with emphasis on how we can gain value for items from their collection and preservation in this way. In the *Vogue* article "The Fight for the Fashion Archive: Brands, Collectors and Gen Z Face Off" we see how brand building has seeped into the social media accounts of devoted fashionistas looking to build their own credibility in the preservation spaces typically controlled by companies. It is fun to consider how we are influenced by the way brands and stores appeal to our own ideas of value. How does visiting a store or business affect how we view that business? How does purchasing an item we see on display in an establishment affect how we view ourselves? We can consider how becoming an owner of a brand's items or visiting a well-known building or restaurant can confer value to us as a people.

The original store for Tiffany and Company is located in New York City on the corner of 57th St. and 5th Avenue. It is a landmark building and represents the moment when Tiffany morphed from being a designer to a retailer of home goods with an eventual and lasting focus on jewelry. Through this example, we can briefly consider branding and its effects on us as consumers and spectators.

On a visit to Tiffany & Co. during the holiday season, I am greeted by a complete 2024 redesign of the building with holiday themes referencing a new setting made for the Tiffany Diamond. As explained in the text accompanying the display of the diamond, "The stone's acquisition solidified the House's reputation as the 'Diamond Kings' and the world's diamond authority . . . The House reset its famed diamond in a new masterpiece to celebrate the grand reopening of its iconic Landmark on Fifth Avenue." The diamond is set in a glass case on the first floor of the store. The repetition of this setting's theme on the walls reinforces the importance of this historical object and reinforces Tiffany's reputation as the preeminent retailer of fine jewelry.

Tiffany employs a number of brand ambassadors at its flagship store that are tasked with greeting visitors, providing history of the brand and location, and even giving tours of the building. Two of these ambassadors were eager to show me around and explain the changes the company has made in recent years. Under its acquisition by the French luxury goods manufacturer LVMH (Louis Vuitton Moet Hennessy), they have doubled down on building their archives and sharing the history of the brand with the public. Acting as preserver of a landmark building, a museum with rotating exhibits, a place for collaboration with artists, and an archive of past works, as well as a place for Instagrammable photos, the mechanics of the building read a lot like a museum/archive, with the difference being that it's a retail store. From the multiple historical items on display to a historic fireplace they brought in through a window to install on the sixth floor, you can see the history of the brand everywhere.

Their larger exhibits show the way they want to be perceived by the public. They have a permanent exhibition of a dinner party à la Judy Chicago by Julian Schnabel. This massive exhibit consists of a dining room set, paintings, and china by the artist. This installation was used for marketing and to embed the brand in a historical and progressive moment. The items inspired by this collaboration and exhibit sold out immediately. The exhibition at the flagship will be permanent.

The Audrey Hepburn Experience one floor down has the original Givenchy dress as well as a reel of the actress in the famous movie *Breakfast at Tiffany's* flanked by two modern portraits of the artist. It is a place to take photos and one of the store's most popular exhibits. Nearby, a first edition of the Truman Capote book along with pencils and annotated pages from the original manuscript are displayed.

Flagship stores such as this one become places not only to purchase goods, but to visit, learn the history of a brand, gain information, and take selfies that you will post online. Here you can even purchase a book on the Tiffany Archives, a thick Tiffany blue volume filled with high-resolution photos of historically important and aesthetically beautiful objects made, preserved, and cataloged by the company.

Outside of the Tiffany & Co flagship, we can see the history of restaurants and businesses throughout New York City and how they use objects to create atmosphere and also brand the importance of the buildings they occupy and flank. The Lever House on Park Avenue ushered in the International Style and is a historical landmark. Sculptures by Claes Oldenburg and Coosje van Bruggen are visible in the courtyard. Hard Rock Cafes built their model on the acquisition and display of celebrity-owned cultural items, and restaurants like Keens in NYC draw people in not just with their food, but with the collection of churchwarden pipes on their walls.

While a flagship store may not be a part of your community, you can take a look at local businesses, chain stores, restaurants, and office buildings that you frequent. Look at where you go to eat, work, and shop and see how those places collect and display objects. How does what's on view inform you about their brand and business model? How does this then affect your relationship to what is being marketed? We can learn a lot by examining objects for sale, how the history of businesses and brands is curated, and what we are encouraged to admire and purchase.

Assignments and Student Examples

Assignment #5 (Informal "Low Stakes")—Institutional Objects

This week, you will be examining an object that is "collected" in an institution. This week's readings will talk about the building of collections, particularly in terms of identity, but your exploration can be broader or different than the authors' specific considerations.

Items that are publicly "collected" in an institution can be viewed many ways; the key is the "collection" must be intentional. That means the institution or business has put thought, time, or money (or any combination of the three) into curating a space full of objects or housing a collection of things that the public can view and/or access.

Archives do this, museums do this, libraries do this, some business buildings in NYC do this, some stores do this in their flagship locations, some restaurants do this, and so on. Think through these suggestions or outside of the box!

For this week, you need to take a picture of an institutionally collected object that is part of an intentional collection by that entity. You want to write a page about the impact this object has on you as an outsider to the institution and post both on this board. You must choose something you can visit in person for this assignment.

Intention of the Assignment

As I mentioned in Chapter 3, I encourage writers to have direct experiences as much as possible for their writing. Like other assignments, you would probably be able to draw on your memories of visiting a museum, library, or other public collection to complete this assignment. Going out into the world and experiencing something in order to write about it changes the way we are able to view and consider our experience.

Since it can be challenging for us to wrap our heads around the idea of institutional objects, I make sure I take my students on a field trip specifically to look at something in person. We discuss the nature of digital archives and accessibility at length, but the point of a lot of our writing is to have interaction with the spaces where objects are situated and consider the materiality and environment, including the people surrounding them and their sensory experiences.

Although our communities can be full of a large range and variety of museums, corporate offices, and stores, students often have not yet ventured to any of these places on their own. This is their chance to visit a space of their choosing rather than just being subjected to my chosen field trips in class for writing.

As a writer, this is a good opportunity to explore your own communities and what they have to offer as well. What do your library's collections look like? What local museums do you have? What is available in terms of public archives? What can you come to understand about your immediate community by what exists in these public-facing collections? How are they presented and accessed? What do they contain, and how is it contextualized and displayed?

This is not a museum studies course. At FIT, we do offer a museum studies curriculum, and it is very valuable if I have students who are studying these concerns in depth in my class. Our purpose with these assignments is to connect to the curated objects in our communities and understand how they influence our ideas of value in our public and personal lives.

Student Example Assignment #5—Institutional Objects

Alexandra Walicke—A Single Present

"Postcard from New Jersey," "the English seaside," "a cartoon drawing of Dad," "me and Ben (my dog) at home," "Mum's mum," "Dad with Uncle Sonny (the Jazz days)," "You wearing stupid glasses."

One Moment in Time (Kitchen) (2002) is an eighty-slide projection of artist Jonathan Monk's mother's kitchen. Well, it's a projection of a transcription describing the objects in the kitchen, not the kitchen itself—and it's not just his mother's kitchen; it's *ours*, too. We can't help but project ourselves into the museum exhibits—I've seen a postcard of New Jersey, too. I've worn stupid glasses, too.

Museums are obsessed with the ephemeral, the fleeting moment. They're obsessed with dying, with preserving.

If these slides are preserved, maybe the kitchen will be, too, long after the photographs and postcards are gone. As if those photographs and postcards themselves weren't trying to capture something and let it last forever.

But you can't cheat death—paper disintegrates, and museum exhibits get replaced with time, too.

So much for modernity, huh? They all claim to be the "now" but there's nothing more "now" than us, viewing the exhibit. It's the pleasure of knowing that we have something over them; we're beating them at their own game.

Though, carved stone is tougher than skin, so that too won't last for long.

In the next room, there is a TV. On it, is Antonio Paucar's *Marcelinho* (2005). You can't take a photo of it without seeing a grid of blue and red, each pixel demanding to be seen—a gentle reminder that it's outdated but still there, too. I love cathode-ray tube TVs and projectors at museums. There is a reverence to outdated, fragile technology, fighting tooth and nail to remain alongside those more modern than themselves.

Antonio,

I'm watching a video of you. You're outside playing with, burning a wheel. The placard tells me Duchamp's readymades inspired you, and you thought of how you played when you were a boy. Is it readymade if you have to burn the wheel yourself? I guess you saw it in real life, in Berlin, and I didn't. So, maybe you know more—you're in the museum and I'm not, after all.

When I see you, I see that you're not a boy playing with this wheel, but you're a man. A man remembering what it's like to be a boy. When the screen flickers black for a second before it replays, I see myself. I'm not a girl anymore, though I remember what it's like too. I think neither of us are ready to grow up.

The placard says this recording is from 2005. I can't imagine how the time since then and now has changed you. It's been eighteen years since you showed us how you remember being a boy.

When you see this piece now, do you think you look young there? Has your hair become more grey? Do you wish you could've performed it when you *were* a boy, so it's the real thing? Do you stop thinking like this with age?

How do you feel? What should I feel?

Best, Alexandra

Museums are obsessed with the ephemeral—a single moment, a collection of moments, a single present. In formalist film theory, a single present implies a lack of past or future—everything that *is* and *was* is present.

Maybe that's a more comfortable place to lay, in a museum where everything is desperate to preserve its presence, well into when it becomes past.

Everything there—including me.

The following is a series of questions I give students before we visit a public collection together to help them think through the experience. I also have them meet with the curator whenever possible.

Assignment #6 (Informal "Low Stakes")—Archive Questions

For next time, please answer the following questions on our questions discussion board:

1. *What can you get from an object in an institutional collection?*
2. *How does the fact that it is collected in your home institution's archives impact how you view the institution?*
3. *What is the context in which you will have to examine one of these objects in an archive? (Think about our readings and discussions when you answer this.)*
4. *What can writing about an archival object convey about you? About the object? About the collection?*
5. *What story do you want to tell?*

Intention of the Assignment

If you work at an institution like I do, you might want to use the resources at your fingertips. What collections or archives does your college or university have? What experts that manage and curate these collections might be available to talk about their experiences with your class?

As teachers, we cannot be experts on all things, so it is important to invite those who are experts into the conversation whenever possible. Within my own institution and outside of it, I have found leaders to be generous and interested in talking to me and my students. Many people in administrative or curatorial positions don't get to have regular contact with students or in-depth conversations with writers who are interested in their collections. Invite them to share their points of view, expertise, and passions. The best way to come to understand an institution's collections is by talking to the people who build and maintain it.

Essay #2 (Formal "High Stakes")—Institutional Collections

For your second formal piece of creative nonfiction writing, I want you to consider the idea of institutional collections and collecting. For this unit, we have considered what goes into creating an institutional collection. Personal inspiration, a desire to educate, a desire to preserve history, confer monetary value, create a legacy, make objects available to a general public for original research, and to establish the importance of a field of study have all been considered. These past 2 weeks you looked at objects from outside institutions (like the New York Public Library and your own research) as well as our own and learned from archivists their reasons for collecting, what a collection means, and how it might be viewed by people outside of the collection.

For our first large piece of writing, you will continue investigating the idea of institutional collections and what is collected and why. You will be working with objects in the New York Public Library collections we visited for this assignment. The most important thing is that the collection or object you choose to write about tells a story to you, perhaps about societal norms, an event, relationships, value, culture, any of the themes the readings have covered or additional themes that imbue the collections with personal storytelling value. Remember, this piece is no different from our first one—it is about telling us a story that is relevant to you and your point of view. The only difference is your object(s) will be something collected by an institution not directly related to you.

Consider what the authors you have been reading are doing in their writing. How can this help you write your own piece? Think about your peers' pieces and comments, what strikes you about their relationship to objects?

The essay should be about four to six pages, double-spaced in its final form. I encourage you to get this first draft as close to completion for our next class where we will do a formal peer review. You will also receive written feedback from me for revision. This piece will have multiple versions so really go for it! The more you get on the page the more we can work with it!

Please include a photograph of the object or objects you chose to write about.

Intention of the Assignment

This assignment can be challenging for writers. They are being asked to wrap their heads around a complicated concept where the entire point of the exercise is to understand objects that are not personally owned. At this point, we have visited multiple archives and spoken to archivists, handled objects in these collections, taken individual trips to view public objects, and considered their meaning for us. It is still a challenge to create an extended narrative that tells a story of one or a larger number of these items.

In so many institutional settings, we never get the context we so crave. Unlike our personal lives, these things don't have automatic meaning and value for us. As we have explored, The Metropolitan Museum of Art is not known for giving copious amounts of context, especially for its permanent collections. The most relevant space for my students in a museum like The Met is likely the Costume Institute. This part of The Met has done a particularly good job (with the help of Anna Wintour) to raise awareness and attendance through rich exhibitions that tie sensory information and narrative together. The Met Gala, with its media coverage and celebrity attendance, augments the visibility of the collections and the cultural and social importance of the exhibitions.

We are a society that now lacks a lot of commonality because of the plethora of information available to us through the internet. We have fewer and fewer shared cultural experiences because more than ever many of us can cater what we consume more closely to what we like and even what we already know. We are more comfortable with what we personally value in our private lives and often more confused by the things our larger institutions indicate we should value. So much of the way we witness institutions is based on a collective social agreement about their importance, and the cultural contract has changed in many ways. Thus we are all left to question—what will these institutional collections mean to our society going forward? What do these spaces offer us as individuals now? Can we find relevance in something that is not made for our eyes? Do we have the stamina as a culture to make the hard connections necessary to continue to value things outside of our regular and immediate experiences? What objects still resonate and why?

Student Example Essay #2—Institutional Collections

Sarah Loose—The Crumbled Remains of the Other Shelley

"I collected bones from charnel-houses and disturbed, with profane fingers, the tremendous secrets of the human frame."

-MARY SHELLEY, *FRANKENSTEIN*

I'm here to talk about bones—not just any bones, but Mary Shelley's vaguely-famous husband's bones, more precisely, though in all honesty, it doesn't matter. Without a label, bones are just bones, after all. Unlike most bones, however, fragments of Percy Florence Shelley's deteriorating remains have been framed and placed within a glass display case, exhibited in the same room as Jefferson's handwritten manuscript of the Declaration of Independence and one of the few remaining copies of the complete Gutenberg Bible. *These* bones, the frame and display case seem to say, are not just *any* bones. *These* bones, the famous relics that surround it whisper through the glass, are *special* bones.

The bones do not *look* like bones. They look like chips of slate, maybe, or perhaps flakes of rusted iron, but nothing about them beyond their label reads as "skull fragments" at first glance (or second, or third . . . honestly, I still have doubts as to whether we know for sure that these are bones). Nevertheless, each piece, even the near-microscopic crumbs, has been carefully spaced out on a piece of white paper so that none of the fragments dare overlap, a visual reminder that these are *special* bones, lest the viewer forget to appreciate each and every individual speck of the less-famous Shelley's dead body.

Now, while Percy Shelley's crumbling bits of skull have achieved far more acclaim than most of those laid to rest six feet under, the soul they once belonged to has been a bit less lucky. The exhibit the bones are placed in, after all, is not one dedicated to the life and accomplishments of Percy Shelley, a famous Romantic poet in his own right. Instead, these skull fragments have been curated by the New York Public Library's Treasures Exhibit for their section dedicated to the life of his widow, Mary Shelley. Alongside the bones, this collection contains letters, manuscripts, and other ephemera that once belonged to the female Shelley, in addition to more contemporary objects that speak to the cultural and literary impact of her most famous publication, *Frankenstein*.

My initial reaction upon seeing the display—or more accurately, upon reading its label, as we've established that these bones are most definitely not identifiable as such on their own—was an innate sense of horror. *Is nothing sacred?* I whispered to myself. *Must we pillage and defile even this?* Of course, this response was fueled in part by an assumption that these bones were collected unethically, an inference colored by the countless stolen bones on display in American cultural institutions acquired via the looting of Indigenous American burial sites, ancient Egyptian sarcophagi, and so on. Percy Shelley's bones, in contrast, were not so much pillaged from his final resting place as they were picked through mid-cremation by a friend. Whether these details alter the morality of the action when Shelley himself never invited such post-mortem treatment, who's to say, but the cultural consensus seems to be that if a *friend* steals your bones, all is fine and dandy. Perhaps another moral justification can be made via a historical relativism argument, as the separation of these skull fragments from the rest of Shelley's skeleton took place during the Victorian Era, a time in which collecting bones (as well as hair, fingernails, and other parts of dead and dying bodies) was a cultural norm, and a reflection of the prevailing attitudes towards death, science, and the human body. But suppose we accept that—circumstantially—the acquisition or collection of human remains can be done ethically. I still must ask; *why*? For all I felt while lingering upon the framed fragments of Percy Shelley's skull was a vague skepticism, paired with a sense that emanating from this object was an importance I was meant to grasp, but that simply escaped me. Should I feel something, looking at these crumbs of a long-gone corpse? Is this supposed to speak to me?

Here, I shall admit that I am not one with a particular passion for Romantic poetry and consequently am generally uninterested in the legacy of Percy Shelley. I am, however, a fan of Mary Shelley, or at the very least, of her novel, *Frankenstein*, which I consider one of my favorite books. In this regard, I suppose I align myself with the NYPL's slight against Percy Shelley in favor of his spouse, as I'd imagine I would not have paused my exploration of the Treasures Exhibit had this case been dedicated to the other Shelley. Yet when I arrived home that evening, it was Percy Shelley's pitiful skull-dust that lingered in the back of my mind as I found myself flipping through my old copy of *Frankenstein*, skimming the pages as if searching for answers in the words of his wife.

Mary Shelley's *Frankenstein* was the first classic I ever fell in love with. Sure, it was also the first I read of my own volition (and the Shakespeare I was required to struggle through in middle school wasn't providing much competition), but nonetheless, upon first picking up the novel, I could think of little else. In it, we follow a doctor (Victor Frankenstein) as he attempts to artificially create life, piecing together human corpses into a living (but deformed) being who, upon being spurned for his appearance, ultimately turns against mankind and his creator. *Frankenstein* had everything I never knew I wanted in a novel: rich symbolism, societal critique, subverted genre conventions, philosophical speculations, and sympathetic monsters—multi-page meditations all set against a backdrop of snowy scenery and harsh mountains.

Flipping through these pages after my visit to the NYPL, I finally realized what had unsettled me so much about the bone fragments. One of the primary themes explored in Mary Shelley's *Frankenstein* is the human obsession with exerting control over that which we do not understand-life, death, creation, and the rest of the world's mysteries. Just as Dr. Frankenstein meticulously assembles his monster from an assortment of stolen human corpses, so too are the NYPL's skull fragments a tangible reminder of this fixation on the unknown and macabre. In the same vein, just as Dr. Victor Frankenstein's pride and scientific curiosity lead him to disturb the natural order (creating life from death), the exhibition similarly disturbs the sanctity of Percy Shelley's remains by reducing them to mere artifacts in a curated spectacle.

The broader question of when it is—and isn't—"okay" to display human remains is a complicated one that can't be answered by focusing on a singular example. The display of these bones, if not a black-and-white example, however, feels, at the very least, to contain a stroke of irony. Alongside Mary Shelley's literary masterpiece, with its themes of creation and moral responsibility, the NYPL museum curators seem oblivious to the symbolism they have placed themselves in, willfully signing up for the role of "mad scientist" without a hint of self-awareness.

5 THINGS WE LEAVE BEHIND

What Is Left and Why

The things we inherit and the things left over from life and living can be the most emotionally burdensome to people. What should we keep and what should we throw away? Where does it go? Where should it go? Can it be useful in some other way? This chapter will consider what is left behind by people and how those things can be critically reflected upon and used to inspire meaningful prose.

Most of us have felt overwhelmed when faced with what is left behind by others, especially if we are tasked with taking care of the stuff. Many of us fear making the wrong choices in what we discard or donate. There is a complex set of emotions that accompanies this kind of decision-making.

We can feel conflicted because we are overcome with emotion, lack time and resources, or don't have the knowledge to make the best decisions about where things end up. Families often feud over inheritances and people become estranged over their relationships to trash and refuse. At this point in my life, I have helped many people sort family heirlooms, gone to hundreds of house sales and auctions, and run estate sales myself. I have witnessed firsthand a broad spectrum of how people live with and accumulate stuff. Since this work has been part of my life since before I can remember, I have developed a skill set for helping others with what is left behind. I am often the person who gives people permission to let go. Many friends and family rely on me to help them sort out not just the stuff but the emotions tied to the things they inherit and must manage.

I have met countless people who have held onto entire homes because they cannot face the burden of the stuff a family member or friend has left behind. I am cautious in valuing things for others since most are disappointed to learn that most stuff has little monetary value. Selling and even donating items can be frustrating and time-consuming. Finding a place for everything in our own homes is difficult and daunting, and businesses are built around our inability to do it. Finding homes and places for someone else's stuff is even harder than dealing with our own things. Taking the time to find the organizations, determine if they will take items, transporting and setting up appointments, sorting what is wanted by you and family members, avoiding drama over possessions, and navigating differences in perceived value of objects can be daunting. It is no wonder people put off dealing with items left behind, trash them, or hire someone else to find them new homes.

Outside of dealing with inheritance, we must face the things we always consider trash. These may be items that don't hold much intrinsic meaning for us and don't bring up all the complicated feelings of inheritance. There is no personal tie to the things, and it is normal in our culture to discard these items once their use is fulfilled. Of course, it turns out our relationship to garbage is much more complicated in other ways.

Students curse me a bit for the main thrust of this section since it makes them look at discarded objects instead of avoiding them. On the congested streets of New York City, most of us make a habit of blocking out as much of the dirt and detritus as possible. There is a palpable stench of urine in the summer, uncollected and rat-infested garbage outside of almost every building, litter on the subway tracks and in the parks, and the overflowing trash cans on street corners that sometimes disappear only to reappear again.

In general, no matter where we live, many of us are rarely forced to face what we discard in our daily lives or we do our best to avoid it. Systems mostly ensure that we can trash things and forget about them. It is a pleasurable feeling to throw something away—out of sight, out of mind. I ask students to notice garbage, their own garbage, the garbage in their daily lives (school, work, homes), and the garbage in the city they inhabit. They are asked to take photos and write about what seeing the trash invokes for them. It is not surprising that facing the garbage we all contribute to can cause distress. Immediately, when sharing, students try to start explaining away what they find in their own trash. This reveals a lot about our relationship to what we throw away.

Once students start noticing the waste around them, they become more curious about investigating what it evokes in them. Around sustainability, students express a lot of anxiety. They have been raised in a world that tells them they should focus on their own environmental impact, perhaps so much so that their instinct is to block out anything they are doing counter to that, which causes them worry.

Working at a school where many students study fashion-related industries, it is hard to ignore the fact that the fashion industry is one of the largest polluters of our planet. In *Fashionopolis: The Price of Fast Fashion & the Future of Clothes*, author Dana Thomas chronicles the changes in fashion production that have led this this outcome. The numbers are astounding to take in: "The Environmental Protection Agency reported that Americans sent 10.5 tons of textiles, the majority of which were clothes, to landfill in 2015. In the UK, 9,513 garments are dumped every five minutes; textiles are the country's fastest-growing waste stream" (Thomas 2019: 8). How can students square their passion for their chosen professions with the realities of its polluting power? It doesn't take long for anyone on social media to see large hauls from fast fashion brands such as Shein and Temu. Students and teachers on campus sport fast fashion. Low cost, staying on trend, and indulging our love of new things are all at play in these systems of production and purchasing. What are the alternatives? And in a world where we are tasked to create the self as brand no matter what our profession, and hauls get clicks, what are the motivations to step back? What are the costs? It's not uncommon for students to pursue these questions or to feel frustrated not knowing what the answers are to solve their conflicting feelings about overproduction, the environment, recycling, and waste.

We can't all change our patterns or take personal responsibility for the waste created on this planet; it's crippling. But by becoming somewhat mindful and noticing our part in it, we can understand our relationship to trash and reused and recycled objects. Many of us are inconsistent with our own practices which is not out of step with the inconsistent practices and messages in larger society. We may carry a reusable water bottle while at the same time being overly reliant on paper cleaning supplies. We might drive an electric vehicle but crank up the air conditioning or heat all year long. We might repurpose and fix certain items that are broken while not wanting to bother with others. Many organizations have stepped in to collect and assist us in reseeing the value of discarded objects for upcycling and creativity. We are only human, and we know corporations bear the brunt of polluting our planet; yet we still must navigate our feelings about what we create.

Even sustainable practices used to curb waste, such as thrifting, which is increasingly enjoyed by a wide range of people, raise ethical questions. Those whom charity and resale shops were initially meant to serve have been priced out of the market by those who may not be shopping because of limited economic means. The resale economy has become readily accessible through easy-to-use sites that can be accessed with smartphones. Our wardrobes have become sources of income, and buying used items has become a way to signal we are sustainably minded while also being fashionable.

In her piece for *British Vogue*, "Should you buy from a thrift store if you can afford not to?" Sophie Benson explores the moral implications inherent in participating in the cycles that perpetuate overproduction and lead to buying second-hand items.

> Ultimately, issues within fashion cannot be separated from issues within wider society. A consumerist system perpetuates a feeling of entitlement to a constant stream of new goods; prices which reflect fair compensation of labour seem cruelly out of reach while wages stagnate; a largely hidden system which transports billions of excess garments to the Global South still upholds a perception of scarcity in order to sell more clothes. Simply put, there is more than enough to go around, but unless we pull back and look at the wider forces at play, just like second-hand clothes, this debate will continue to circulate. (https://www.vogue.co.uk/fashion/article/is-thrifting-ethical)

While singular actions and shopping habits cannot fix a larger problem, examining our part in these cycles can help us understand the bigger cultural models that enable the overproduction of goods that leads to waste.

Refuse, detritus, clutter, inherited objects, and other evidence of life and living surround us. What do we make of these objects? What can they inspire us to write? How can we square ideas of sustainability and our obsession with objects? What happens to our objects when we die? What do we recycle, upcycle, and throw away, and why? Many modern objects are meant to be discarded instead of cherished. We are encouraged to clear away our clutter and live simply. Brands trash items to maintain exclusivity and control markets. Generational and cultural ideas of object value influence what is kept and what is thrown away. Here we will look at waste and those objects left behind. Much has been written on waste and waste studies is an ever-growing field. How can we apply this to examining what we and the people around us throw away and leave behind? Topics that will be considered include but are not limited to: cultural notions of waste, waste and discard studies, inherited objects, waste as art, and changing fads that influence what we need and keep.

Inherited Objects

The complications of object inheritance are a more familiar subject for some than for others. It might be the case that you have never experienced the death of a loved one or if you have, you were not put in a position to directly deal with what was left behind. If you inherited something, it might have been through the mediation of a relative who presented you with a few things to remember a person by. You may have received a gift from a relative before they passed or you may have only witnessed your family and friends dealing with the possessions of those who have died.

We may have a lot of happy memories associated with the possessions we received after the passing of a loved one, while many of us may feel emotionally and physically burdened by these things. The items may make us remember the love we shared with the person or special moments that we spent together. Cherished objects may be displayed in our homes, worn on our bodies, or put away to be kept safe. These objects may spark conversations with others, bring up memories, or commemorate a special moment we shared with the person. These are the few items that are sorted out because they are desired and already have complex meanings to us. Beyond treasured items, there are many other remnants of life and living that come along with the end of it.

For those of us who have dealt with death and mortality and the objects we inherit, this writing will evoke a lot of feelings. What does it mean to want something of someone else's once they have passed? What does it mean to own the object ourselves and how does its meaning change with the change in ownership?

In her book *Objects of the Dead: Mourning and Memory in Everyday Life*, Margaret Gibson conducts a series of interviews with Australian individuals who have suffered loss. In her chapters, she breaks down how her subjects make sense of what they are tasked to deal with, finding certain categories of items are usually treated similarly while there is wide variation in others.

> No one in the interviews had any qualms about selling most household effects, but no one said that they would sell the clothes of a deceased family member. The decisions made about the fate of objects revealed a moral system whereby monetary gain should be made only on certain types of objects and under certain conditions; for example, I discovered that most personal objects become "gifts" to family and friends or donations to strangers through the charity economy, though it may be morally acceptable to sell clothing when poverty or financial need is an issue. Time, and emotional, relational, or generational closeness to the deceased, may alter this general moral standard and code of behaviour. Thus, in terms of conscience, jewellery could be sold more easily when the seller was of another generation or an emotionally or genealogically distant kin. (Gibson 2008: 4–5)

The way that people consider these different objects and what they feel comfortable selling and disposing of has a lot to do with the person's relationship to the deceased as well as their own system of values. For most of us, certain items are different because they were owned by someone who, in this case, we intimately know. We see this come up again and again in the chapters of this book.

> Buying a dress, a shirt, jeans, shoes, a book, a saucepan, glassware—any number and type of object—involves the transference of that object from the market setting of the shop to the setting of the home. The image of the object in the shop, its lure as something of practicality, desire, status or identity, is also transferred, not necessarily without change, to the home. However, when an object loses "newness" because it has been touched and possessed, it may also lose its lure as a commodity; of course, this depends on the object and the owner. (Gibson 2008: 11)

In other words, once something is purchased, the nature of the item changes. Sometimes, once the thrill of the purchase is gone, there is little charm to the item. On the other hand, ownership confers a certain amount of importance on even relatively unimportant items. For instance, when my grandmother passed away, I kept a chipped bowl she used daily to make salads. While the object itself has no monetary value, it is a special item to me because it reminds me of my grandmother cooking in the kitchen, carefully preparing nightly meals for us. I can imagine the moments we spent together making and eating the salad, and it always makes me happy to use the bowl for my own cooking. It is one of my favorite things that I inherited from my grandmother, much more valuable than other items like pieces of jewelry that have more monetary value.

What all of this means is that most of the objects we choose to keep and display have sentimental meaning and complex associations that add value to the object. These are the pieces we might visit on a regular basis, while items with more monetary value might be stored away for a rainy day.

Even if you have not been directly affected by the death of a loved one, we can come to understand feelings about what is left behind and rituals of death because we as a society have a shared traumatic touchpoint in the COVID pandemic. This was a moment where we were all forced to consider mortality and also publicly witness what it was like when people were not able to take part in the processes of death and dying. In the 2021 CCN article, "COVID-19 took away their last moments together. Now families cherish what was left behind," Marisa Gerber explores through photography and interviews what those who lost loved ones inherited after their passing.

Objects grabbed quickly for COVID patients who were rushed to the hospital for care were both useful and random, only to ultimately become poignant reminders of the loved ones' final moments. For Jennifer Lloyd, whose father was rushed to the hospital, she grabbed a number of practical items: "his cellphone, wallet, hairbrush, toothbrush and a set of pajamas" (Gerber 2021). He was one of the first to die during the pandemic.

> When she picked up his belongings the next day, hospital staffers told her to spray everything with Lysol, but she couldn't handle the thought of destroying any lingering scent. A few days later, she went into the basement of her father's home by herself and opened the bag. She took a deep breath, inhaling his Aqua Velva aftershave. (Gerber 2021)

Jennifer continued to text his cellphone as well and listen to his voice messages. We can see through this touching example and others in the reading that the things left behind from the dead can carry a lot of emotional weight. The sensory value of the objects is often important to the person who inherits them, capturing more ephemeral remnants and evidence of the person's life and being. We often keep things that were close to the body of the person we have lost or that capture a sense of their personality and quirks.

The only thing I kept of my father's after his death was a winning scratch-off lottery ticket he had in his wallet. Of all things, this made me smile and think of happier times. There was something about the scratched nature and minimal value of the item that was in his wallet that made it more important to me.

We can consider a wide range of events, from natural disasters to uprisings and war that bring together communities and demonstrate what is truly important and valued by those left behind. COVID was a rare time when the entire world was united around a pandemic and how we viewed objects could be understood from a global as well as personal perspective.

One of the only other pieces of fiction I use in my course other than the Margaret Atwood in Chapter 3 is excerpts from Tim O'Brien's book, *The Things They Carried.* Much like the Atwood piece, I find the cataloging of items to be evocative. O'Brien chronicles the things carried by men on their backs through the Vietnam War, from the sentimental to the functional, making us consider as readers what simple objects meant to them in the worst of conditions, and how their relationship to these items changed as their circumstances did. When some of the men died, their fellow soldiers were left to make sense of their objects. In his fiction, O'Brien uses the categorization of these items to make sense of the individual and communal loss that comes with war.

Inheritance may be a time of sorting and donation, taking stock, and making decisions about what makes sense to move and what should be left behind. It also may be a time to closely examine what we and others have kept over the years. When we put off the decision-making, the burden of things and what to do with them gets passed down to another generation and another. There is no wonder that we feel relief throwing something away and never considering where it goes. There is too much stuff and at some point we have decision fatigue and just want to move on. The emotional ties to these things, which can be fond reminders of time spent with loved ones, can also impose a psychic burden on us that is hard or impossible to escape. Like breaking up with a bad partner, we may just feel better when we cut and run, or we may forever feel obligated to freeze a moment in time before the person passed.

Personal Waste and Cultural Values

In class, we discuss how the concept of garbage and waste is all relative to the individual and the worlds they inhabit. In previous chapters of this book, I have talked about the valuation of things by individuals and also their compulsions to keep, acquire, or collect things. Waste and refuse and their definitions fall on a spectrum and have a lot to do with perspective. What we value can be seen through a cultural lens and be related to societal values as well as socioeconomic conditions. Many industries create massive amounts of waste through production. The fashion industry, something my institution is heavily invested in, as I have mentioned, is responsible for heavily polluting our planet. Like most institutions, my home college has worked hard to join the fight for sustainability, developing curriculum and programming to discuss what can be done. I serve as a member of the President's Council on Sustainability, which is a group of professors, administrators, students, and staff who are committed to sustainable practices, programming, and curriculum.

Countless studies and documentaries have come out looking at the cost of mass production in terms of human labor and materials and what happens to them at the end of their life cycles or if they are never sold. In many of the dumpster diving and thrifting videos I mentioned watching earlier, there is copious evidence showing companies throwing away good food and objects, trashing items that are opened and returned, or forcing employees to cut and destroy designer objects so that the ones in the marketplace don't lose value. What we are told we can recycle versus what we are actually able to recycle doesn't always match up either. The United States has policies that force other countries to take or buy our waste, especially from plastic and textiles, which in turn can overwhelm entire communities and ecosystems.

There are many reminders of the waste our habits are creating. I recently showed my students part of the documentary on the clothing brand Brandy Melville, *Brandy Hellville and the Cult of Fast Fashion*. As a part of the documentary, we see footage of the clothing waste that is shipped to Ghana, poisoning its people and water supply. I ask my class after we finished watching if seeing this footage and interviews with people would make them stop buying from the company. My students said they still appreciated the items from the brand even while they were shocked by the footage and the company's participation in wasteful practices. For many of us, it is too overwhelming to take in the scale of this problem or perhaps we have by necessity become numb to our carbon footprint because systems in place help us to deny it.

In her book *Unraveled: The Life and Death of a Garment*, Maxine Bédat chronicles the sourcing, production, and waste that goes into clothing manufacture. She does this with a focus on the most American of textiles: denim. "When I set out to write Unraveled, I wanted to trace the life and death of a single pair of jeans—a garment that is ubiquitous in our culture, beloved for function and style alike—from farm to landfill" (Bédat 2021: xiv). This book shows how much of fashion's production practices are hidden, unknown, and masked and what it truly means to be transparent about the waste in the fashion industry. Most of us, even those involved in production, may not know the processes of manufacture, and hiding waste to reduce the burden is intentional.

It is hard to wrap our heads around the systems that produce waste and how we offload what is leftover onto others to deal with. While I cannot give a comprehensive overview of waste and the fields of waste and discard studies, quickly evolving fields that are trying to capture the sociopolitical and historical implications of what we produce and throw away, I can share some perspectives on how we can begin to consider the waste in our own lives and some ideas that my students and I have found intriguing when applied to our own writing and lives.

I encourage students to consider their personal roles in the systems we study and write about. We may not want to see ourselves as the bad person in the narrative, and that is okay, but we all play a role in the systems in which we live in big and small ways. Our writing assignments are a way for us to understand our participation in these cycles of valuation and production and to see what personal ways we connect to our place in the life cycle of objects. Our realizations might not always be the most pleasant, and we can drown in justifications for our participation. No matter what the outcome, it will help us to deepen our reflection if we are able to truthfully observe and understand our relationship to what is left behind.

In the introduction to their book, *Culture and Waste: The Creation and Destruction of Value*, editors Gay Hawkins and Stephen Muecke introduce the emotions waste causes individual people.

> Our feelings about waste can signal the plurivocity of being, the ways in which we are inextricably connected to that which we so often want to eliminate and escape. The relational and its connective power is

> where things happen; it is an in-between, a potential line of flight. There is the political possibility of affect as a response where different becomings might emerge—without such responses there can be no ethics of responsibility. The intensities that many of the chapters in this collection describe reveal not our difference from waste and our mastery of it, but our professional implications with it. (Hawkins and Muecke 2002: xiv)

Waste cannot be conquered, but it can be studied and understood. We can consider our own practices of facing what we produce and hiding from it. We can make ourselves aware of the different kinds of waste that occupy our world.

From the descriptions above, it seems trash is all gloom and doom. To be sure, waste is an emotionally heavy topic. I want to mention that beyond these considerations, looking at a trash can also be fun and interesting. When my spouse and I moved into our first house together, a tear down from 1780, we were overwhelmed with the work of repairing a property with a huge hole in its roof and squirrels living inside. For a break, we spent an entire rainy afternoon digging through an old garbage pile we found in the woods.

It was not uncommon for people to create garbage dumps on their own land before the modern waste elimination structures we know today were put into place. The rusted enamel pots, porcelain shards, jars, old bottles, and mattress springs seemed magical to me. We dug deeper and deeper in the mud and leaves, laughing at the random objects that came to the surface. I marveled at the history I inherited from the owners before us, and it all came to me through their garbage. I thought of the generations of people who had occupied the house and what their lives were like. I had dreams of what I would do with things I found. I displayed a few of the hundreds of jars in our entryway and put flowers in one on our kitchen table. Most of the objects ended up moved to the dilapidated barn, waiting for the next owners to fulfill their imaginary potential now that they had been unearthed.

This is one of my happiest memories from our house, and it is one focused on refuse. There is something deeply human about what we throw away and discard. After our day of digging, I found forums online of people who make a hobby of diving into these old dumps for bottles and pieces of history. While this won't be my full-time hobby, it was a marvel to feel tangible remnants of lives lived there before me. Without those items, the prior owners would be much more like ghosts to me.

Digging through other people's trash can be an intimate exercise and one that also goes too far. While we can learn a lot about others based on what they threw away, there is also a limit to what garbage can reveal. In "*Bob Dylan Is Having a Hollywood Moment. His No. 1 Hater Is Ready,*" we get a reminder of the dangerous boundaries that can be crossed when accessing something so intensely personal.

> In the 1960s, A.J. Weberman became obsessed with Bob Dylan and ultimately viewed him as a traitor to the 1960s counterculture. When Dylan denied his conversation, Weberman turned to the singer's garbage.
>
> He said, "You're not going to get into my life," and he slammed the door, so I figured I'd look through his garbage. Amid dirty diapers and kitchen scraps, he found personal letters and family photographs from the household, where Dylan lived with his wife, Sara, and their young children. I said, "This isn't a garbage can, this a gold mine," he said. (Kilgannon 2025)

He interpreted the findings from Dylan's garbage and made them public, using the disposed items to wage a public war on the musician. There is something interesting in the consideration of exactly how personal garbage can be, what it can and can't reveal about a person and how it can even be weaponized to prove a point.

While looking at trash most likely won't reach obsessive levels for the average person, we can see the personal affect in discarding things that are personal to the home. Taking a topic such as children's art can drive home the emotional nature of throwing things away that we once valued and what they can reveal. In the Object Lessons piece, "Throw Your Children's Art Away," Mary Townsend talks about confronting the large output of creative pieces made by her children and what she should do with them.

> After a few years, I had a crisis over what to do with it all. I hadn't yet started the carefully curated collection that I remember my own mother making for me. And in truth, it's difficult to choose which pieces to keep. "Oh, but we have to keep this one," I think, every single

time. And if this one, why not another? Eventually, I started throwing it all away. Perhaps I am a monster. But the relief involved leads me to believe I'm onto something. What parents do with children's art depends on what they think about the nature of childhood, nostalgia, and beauty. The correct answer is to make the art, bestow it upon someone to behold and admire for a while, and then toss it. It makes the right tribute to beauty and it's the correct moral stance toward the more ephemeral qualities of childhood. (Townsend 2018: 2)

Sometimes the throwing away is a positive thing. We can recognize the evidence of a moment in time, one that can never be preserved, and take joy in the things that come from it. We can also let it go.

When I was a young Master's student, I went to see Kurt Vonnegut speak. In his snarky tone, the bitterness of nonconformity permeating all of his words to us, he said that if we were real writers we should be able to put something to paper and then throw it away. There's something right about this. Townsend's piece echoes this thought of Vonnegut's in a poetic way. "It's the act of *making* the art that's useful and good for children, then let this part of the art live, and then let its results die" (Townsend 2018: 5). The interest in a lot of writing, like the making of waste, can also be in the process and understanding how it came to be, not the result itself.

Doing a Trash Audit

Each semester I ask my students to do a self-waste audit and to take a look at the waste they generate in a day. Waste audits can be completed at a workplace or at home. In my class, I ask them to do a little of both—look at their personal life and the worlds they inhabit at school and in the broader city. This can be a painful exercise for anyone because the act of throwing something away in and of itself is satisfying and makes us feel like we are in control of our environment. Having to face the waste we create can be overwhelming and make us feel defeated. On our campus, which is in the heart of midtown New York City, it is probably not surprising that the majority of the waste is food-related, the most prevalent waste being coffee cups.

Convenience is a big factor, especially with the hectic lives of the average person, and convenience foods especially generate a lot of waste. Students often take seven to eight classes, work and intern, and stay late in studios after regular school hours to finish projects. They discuss how, even if they wanted to, they could not load up on enough caffeine to get them through their days, so they buy these things, then they throw them away. We talk about the pressures of life and living for students and anyone who leads a busy life filled with activities and obligations. We rely on accessibility in order to get through the other things that need to be done.

Convenience often breeds waste, especially in terms of food. Having the time and money to devote to concentrating only on the waste you generate is not a reality for most people. Time is a luxury; getting to choose where and how and what you eat is a luxury. Even composting, a new initiative in New York City, can be a luxury in a small studio with no kitchen space. We talk about what it means to collect food scraps in spaces without wiggle room, known for harboring rats and cockroaches, perhaps without freezers, let alone freezer or counter space. Having choices—something I teach in all of my classes—is a luxury. So much is perpetuated by big brands to defray responsibility and put it on the consumers.

What is our garbage made of? What does it look like to us and what does it mean to actually face it, think about it, and assess it? Can it be interesting or instructive? What does it say about us, how we think about these things, and what does it say about our communities and what we value?

Reduce, Reuse, Recycle

On a weekday, I visit Materials for the Arts, MFTA, a New York City Department of Cultural Affairs program whose mission is to connect artists and educators who do nonprofit work with donated materials for creative reuse. Contained in its warehouse are items leftover from large companies and organizations. The purpose of this program is to keep the items from the trash bins. In line, I meet a fellow professor from another arts institution who has gotten all of his office supplies and furniture from the warehouse. He uses the resources to provide materials to educators in training who do public arts work. Behind me is a woman who does all of the stagecraft for a local theater company. She has three full carts of plastic Halloween bones and rolls of fabric. She tells me that she has outfitted as much as 90 percent of a production with these donated materials and has the joy at the end of a show of returning them to the warehouse for reuse by others.

I am impressed by the wide range of artists and volunteers who rummage purposely through the approximately 5,000 square feet of space filled with everything from paper goods and books to furniture, materials, mannequins, and buckets of paint. People excitedly celebrate what they've unearthed, and volunteers are available to help you find what you need. There is an energetic and frenetic buzz as people push full carts of tulle and lift boxes of supplies. I have come just to observe for future field trips with students, yet I still walk away with a too-heavy pile of books and paper supplies to carry back to school on the subway. As everyone tells me, I should've brought a car.

The importance of identifying recycling centers and reuse centers in your own communities cannot be overstated. It can be overwhelming to be faced with the runoff of businesses and organizations at places like MFTA. It can be equally inspiring to consider how we can keep items out of the trash and put them to good use instead. Saving money, helping keep things out of landfills, and becoming inspired by the objects available to us—these are just some of the ways reusing and recycling items can become a part of our stories.

In Putnam County, New York, you can find a remnant of an earlier time in the Kent Recycling Center. At this 100 percent volunteer-run site, you sort out your recyclables into over thirty categories with the help of neighbors, some of whom were the original founders of the program. They have a free store where you can drop off unwanted goods and take even more home. Community centers like this exist in very few places, mostly because it is unlikely that we have the time or inclination to so carefully sort our leftovers with such a strong team of people to support us. At the same time, I made more friends in this space than anywhere else in my community.

These centers with the recycled and abandoned objects they contain can inspire us to understand not just the local lifecycles of our unwanted items, but also the lifecycles of our global economies alongside the formal and informal ways we can encourage recycling and reuse. Many of us may have been involved in upcycling clothing or items in our lives for creative reuse. A lot of the media surrounding us celebrates repurposing what we have on hand to create better lives. Yet, as we have discussed, we may not be aware of the processes which brought them to our hands in the first place, many of which may influence our drive to keep them out of landfills and find a new space for them in our lives. In *Material Culture and Creative Writing Pedagogy: A Case for "Garbage Land" (in Real Time and Space)*, author Christine Wiesenthal talks about her move to materiality in her writing classrooms, and what students can gain from interacting directly with discarded objects. For this essay, she focuses on her work with waste and waste management and taking students on field trips to different waste management centers. "As part of the assignment connected to our visit, I asked students to select one recyclable object, examine it closely, and subsequently attempt to trace the lifecycle and travels of its component parts, from their point of origin at manufacture to their point of final destination as recycled commodities" (Wiesenthal 2016: 196–7). This connects students to the global economy of waste and recycling and encourages writing that places them within the cycle of reuse, thus inspiring them to think of final destinations for their own items.

When we feel an object has served its purpose in our personal lives, we are left with a series of decisions about what to do next. Do we donate the item? Do we give it to a friend or family member? Should it be thrown away? Or do we think we might need it for something else down the road? Can we make it into something new? Perhaps we are paralyzed by indecision and just put it in a drawer or closet because we can't deal with the decision at the moment. I ask students to look around them and take note of something they have reused and/or repurposed. What we decide to repurpose and why is highly individualized. The process of reuse can be satisfying, but it can also cause anxiety. There is always a danger—if we keep this object for future use, why not others? What is the potential in an object that no longer serves its original function?

We all have containers, closets, drawers, and storage spaces that hold objects we no longer know the purpose of in our lives. These items can be intense burdens for some of us, making us feel disorderly or cluttered. They can remind us of purchases we made that didn't work out or our inability to organize our belongings and prioritize function over other considerations.

Most of us have also have a broken or damaged object that we then kept in one of these spaces. The breaking of an item can cause a lot of pain and a great sense of loss, and we may want to both hold onto the thing and not be reminded of it simultaneously. Growing up in the antiques business, I had a set of rules for avoiding breakage laid out by my parents.

They told me to always throw myself under something fragile if it falls since the human body can heal, but the object cannot.

I was reminded of the pain of losing a favorite object the other day walking down the street. There was the anguished wail of a toddler in a stroller behind me and the words of their parent that they would "buy them another one." Sometimes, a replacement doesn't work—we develop attachment to items because of our history with them and their imperfections. If something we love is lost, can it really be replaced? And if we damage something we cherish, should we keep it in its damaged state or is it too painful to the point that we need it out of our sight? Is there a way to repair it and be satisfied with the outcome?

It's not just cherished objects we have to negotiate these boundaries with. We may have something that is still working or perfectly functional but not in the condition it once was. Do we patch it and continue using it? Is there shame associated with having an imperfect item? Do we want an excuse to buy something new?

I am a huge fan of the BBC show *The Repair Shop*, where individuals bring in objects that have been overly loved or neglected and a team of experts gives them new life. More than a few times, the show has brought me to tears as there is a sense of pride and connection in rescuing these items that have meaning for us. In each episode, the repairs are lovingly carried out by professionals, their processes laid bare so we can see the care and time that goes into the mending.

For most of us when we fix things, we might be inclined to hide the mends as they can be indicators that an object is broken and has lost its value. In the antiques business, it is not uncommon for repairs to paintings, china, and glass to be hidden by paint or fillers. On the other end of the spectrum, there are entire fields of art and collecting devoted to mending the broken and finding the beauty in what is repaired. Japanese Kintsugi uses gold and silver to mend cracks in broken china and porcelain, creating an altered but beautiful object in the process. Chinese Juci used metal staples to join broken porcelain back together and has inspired many collectors and museum exhibitors who celebrate the beauty in the mends. Japanese Sashiko stitching reinforces weaknesses in garments and is also a decorative art form that is openly displayed on clothing. The way we approach the reuse and repair of objects can say a lot about our cultural experience and values and what we can learn from the upcycling or repair of a functional or treasured item.

We may also consider how waste leftover from making functional or artistic objects can inspire reflections. I visited Printed Matter's Art Book Fair in Chelsea in 2024, where a wide range of publications were self-reflective on the trash created during bookmaking. In their *Book Waste Book*, Temporary Services takes a look at what is wasted when printing books. After a discussion about a printing mistake, the authors began a deeper conversation about what to do about it—keep the mistake or dispose of the many pages. "Ultimately the page with an error went into our bindery's recycling bin. The wasted ream raised a bunch of questions for us about our printing practices and how they have changed over the years. The paper was never repurposed for anything in our art, but it triggered a deeper conversation" (Temporary Services 2022: 11). The book is a product of this conversation about decision-making and waste practices in book printing. The authors explain the layers of making left behind in typical runs with their Risograph copiers. "We often use our test copies to absorb this particularly heavy ink for the first prints. Each of us maintains piles of these overprinted pages—more than four vertical feet of paper in Chicago alone. Over time, they have accumulated the history of things we've made with the machines" (Temporary Services 2022: 13). These pages are objects that show how things are made, without much intrinsic value of their own. To address the larger scope of the conversation in the book, the authors decided to include some of these otherwise abandoned pages. "Two examples of these pages have been bound inside this publication. They document our waste, but also make each publication unique through their many variations produced over at least five years of work" (Temporary Services 2022: 13). In this way, they have reused the waste of production as something instructive but also beautiful for the reader, bearing the marks of how things are created.

In "Trash as Archive, Trash as Enlightenment," Patricia Yaeger discusses the long history of trash being made into art and used for political protest. In her essay, she explores how "The project of making trash out of art and art out of trash has a long pedigree" (Yaeger 2002: 104) and what we can learn from looking at rubbish in literature and artistic production that complicates how we view value in repurposing. From mainstream to outsider art, sculpture to film, Yaeger examines case studies that demonstrate that this repurposed trash is "a mess with a message" (Yaeger 2002: 114).

Beyond artistic repurposing, we can see everyday people finding creative ways to reuse trash to create different meanings. In *The Afterlife of Discarded Objects: Memory and Forgetting in a Culture of Waste*, authors Andrei Guruianu and Natalia Andrievskikh break down how we culturally assess items as either valuable or disposable. They look to life in post-communist Russia and Romania to understand how the objects left over developed new meanings and were repurposed by people looking to invent new ways of life.

> The abrupt turn to consumerism during the 1990s after decades of poverty and repression changed people's perception of the material world around them. Inspired by these conversations, in 2014 we launched The Afterlife of Discarded Objects, where we solicited and subsequently archived contributors' memories about playing with, preserving, or making art from what we might broadly label as trash, waste, or unwanted, discarded items. (Guruianu and Andrievskikh 2018: 3)

Their website and book feature images and stories of these items that highlight the repurposing of objects after cultural and political change and the stories these people and objects have to tell. As we have discussed throughout this book, objects and how we interact with them can reveal the intimate ways we operate in and consider the world around us. This is universally true.

> Whether our contributors came from Italy, Kuwait, the United States, Russia, or India, and whether they submitted poems, brief recollections or well-developed nonfiction narratives, one aspect of their shared memories stood out as common ground. While writing about their action and relationship with objects they seemed to reveal at the same time something about themselves: their own personal views toward material objects, the way value is constructed and attributed to things, and their particular society's attitudes toward waste. (Guruianu and Andrievskikh 2018: 3–4)

We can reveal shifts in cultural attitudes toward value as well as come to understand how we change and evolve in what we see value in through this kind of examination. What we once valued may have a new function or no function in our lives. We may devote time to rescuing detritus, mending and upcycling the objects in our lives, or be inclined to discard what we no longer want to deal with.

Assignments and Student Examples

Assignment #7 (Informal "Low Stakes")—Objects of the Dead

For next week's homework, I am asking everyone to post a picture of an object they inherited from someone who has passed away. If you do not have an object from someone who passed away, please ask friends or family members if they have an object with a story and photo they would like to share. We will be spending next class discussing these objects. You do not need to write for this assignment.

Intention of the Assignment

As I mentioned above, inheritance can be a difficult topic for writers for a whole host of reasons. This is the only assignment where I ask students to provide only a photo or series of photos of objects they would like to discuss with a class. I find this to be a Low Stakes way for them to enter what can be an emotionally challenging subject.

I spend time projecting their submitted digital images on the board and invite each student to share the importance of the object with their peers. This creates a shared experience among the class and doesn't assess the value of the object for the audience. This process instead allows students a safe way to dip their toes into an idea that often yields their most layered writing at the end of our class together. We get to share memories and show how people are valued through their objects in funny and sentimental ways by those who loved them.

Assignment #8 (Informal "Low Stakes")—Trash

This week's assignment asks you to look at trash! Trash, for our purposes, is a collection of things discarded by humans, so keep this definition in mind. There is so much trash to choose from in so many locations in the city—in regular old garbage cans, schools, dumpsters, collection sites, public parks, tourist spots, businesses, art establishments, restaurants, grocery stores, subways, and so on. Be creative! Take a few pictures of your trash to share with the class!

Intention of the Assignment

As mentioned above, we can all be very resistant to looking at trash; it's gross! Especially in New York City, we are surrounded by foul smells and foul sights. From excrement to old food, most of us want to hide from all of the waste we are surrounded by. This assignment asks us to do the opposite; not only should we not ignore the garbage, we should photograph it, interact with it, look more closely, think about and describe it, and how it makes us feel. Luckily, you don't need to live in a city to be surrounded by refuse and detritus; it's everywhere!

It's important to confront that which we usually find objectionable. This can have larger theoretical implications and help with harder subjects that we may want to avoid. It can also just help us understand that which we purposefully put aside, hide from, and why.

Student Example Assignment #8—Trash

Eliza Wicks—Trash

The strangest part about living in New York City is remembering that it is a community. A very large and not always friendly community, but one nonetheless. I always remember this whenever there is some big event or phenomenon that occurs and it seems as though the whole city stops and for a short while, we're just one big family sharing an experience together.

The earthquake was one. Not even five minutes later, Twitter and TikToks were already poking fun at the shocking yet inconsequential event, with people from all boroughs giving their commentary as if we were all in the same room as it happened.

The second and probably bigger one was the eclipse. Granted, it felt the whole country stopped for a few days to admire this event, but it felt especially big in New York. Not even 3 days before, I hadn't even heard that there was anything happening and suddenly it was all that I could hear. The day didn't feel much different than any other and I went about my normal activities, rushing around to get various assignments done to maybe get a chance to watch the eclipse if I had the time.

Twenty minutes before the peak time started, I pushed my way down 5th Ave, determined to get in and out of Banana Republic and back to school before it was time. I couldn't believe how many people were out and about on a Monday, people that had likely traveled to New York precisely for the event. The sidewalks were almost unwalkable, everyone looking up at the sky instead of in front of them, stopping and standing here and there. Madison Square Park was filled, people spilling out onto the sidewalks and streets. In all of my time in New York City, this was one of the most remarkable things I have seen. Instead of taking pictures of the sky, I snapped shots of the people I saw, packed together and milling around like an ant colony in search of their queen. On my way back to school as it got closer and closer to peak time, the air felt frenzied and strange. Workers ran out of their shops and restaurants to crane their necks upwards, most with their own set of flimsy viewing glasses, their efficacy still questionable in my mind.

But not even six hours later, the streets were back to their normal calm chaos. Everyone who had stopped their day for this rare event were once again following their usually scheduled programming, the events of earlier long forgotten.

The only reminder along the long avenue of the hours of commotion and public attention was a pile of trash bags set out on the curb, labeled "Eclipse Glasses." It had occurred to me earlier, as I passed person after person, all donning a similar pair of cardstock glasses, that someone must be profiting big off of the whole ordeal. After all, is it really a cultural event if there isn't a product to be made for it? Just to be easily disposed and forgotten for whatever new thing pops up on their feed.

The magnitude of the amount of waste generated in that one day suddenly hit me and I couldn't help feeling slightly sad. For all of the wonder and amazement of earlier was now replaced with a guilt that I couldn't shake. And I remembered that I am simply a mere cog in the grand old capitalist machine.

Assignment #9 (Informal "Low Stakes")—Reduce, Reuse, Recycle!

For this week, please take a look at something you have repurposed in your life. It can be something that once was used for something else and is now used for something new, something that you rescued and reused in your home, something you have upcycled, or something that serves a different function than was originally intended. Be creative! Take a photo a write a couple of pages about what this reuse means to you.

Intention of the Assignment

This tends to be a lighter assignment in a heavier section of the class. Having students take a look at their immediate living conditions, like they did in Assignment #1, to find things they have reused is a bright spot among the darker, heavier themes here. It is a moment to feel good about oneself or to bask in our own ingenuity or creativity.

I get great satisfaction from upcycling and reusing things that might otherwise seem valueless to someone else. It is a topic that, when explored, can inspire others to do the same with items in their own lives. It is also a very relevant topic for business and design students who, from economic necessity and for the sake of creativity and sustainability, often repurpose materials in their projects for school and work.

Student Example Assignment #9—Reduce, Reuse, Recycle!

Lyla Stratton—My Desk

My desk is simple. It's not antique, with an oak top that turns upwards, revealing a beautiful bundle of old notebooks and sharpened pencils. It doesn't have a special story, like someone's initials inscribed on the bottom like the wooden walls in *Madeline* with some school children's mark, 1910 etched next to 'LS' which I would share how special, this person shared my initials!

No, my desk is a mass manufactured, easily sticky, dusty, white Ikea desk.

I have always wanted a space of my own. Where I could sit, to write, to read and hide my little intricacies in my very own desk. Growing up with my sister, we always shared. We did our homework on Thursday nights, the sun setting long before we sat down to do our studies. Our elbows ached from leaning forward, scribbling in our multiplication tables. It was the same table we have always sat at. Me, 2 years old, chomping on a fruit loop Rice 'Kristie' Bar while my mom left to work the State Fair or carving pumpkins, the wood below us becoming slick with orange goo. We would sit, and work, together on our kitchen table.

And there is a beautiful thing of togetherness, but there is also beauty in having something that is *yours*.

My New York room is small. It does not have a closet. The window opens directly to the trash courtyard, facing a black brick wall. There is no natural sunlight. But it is mine. I can only fit my wardrobe, my bed, and a bookcase. There is no desk to write. And this is fine. I can go sit at the table in the living room, my books sprawled before me, my sister sipping her cappuccino on the armchair next to me.

But still I yearned. My mom would ask me: "What would you do with a bigger room?" "A desk." I said, immediately.

We pondered this, trying to find a space where I could even squeeze a fold out table with a small stool. Nothing.

Until, when we were walking home from dinner, tipsy from a tad more red wine than necessary we stumbled upon my desk. It was dirty. There were brown stains from someone's iced coffee cup in the morning and dust covering the legs. It was buried among trash bags. I questioned for just a moment, thinking, "I can find something better, more special, more beautiful for a real desk." But my mom talked me out of it. She said "Come on! We'll spruce her up? What does it have missing? Look, it even has a fold out drawer."

This got me thinking. Oh, I can put the current book I'm reading there, my notebooks on that end, some pencils below. I did the calculations in my head.

"Okay. Yeah. We just gotta clean it first." (Duh, Lyla)

And that is how I brought my mass-produced, discarded, nothing wrong with it, generic Ikea desk home. During the day, it stays tucked under our 'mantelpiece', you can hardly see it. But during the day, as I sit now, I pull my desk out. I scoop up a handful of pencils and open my laptop, sprawl out all my notebooks and I write. I don't know whose desk this was before me, I don't know how long I will have this desk among all other pieces in my life. But my generic, new, nothing cute desk is special because it is mine. And I saved it. I was there for it to find me.

Essay #3 (Formal "High Stakes")—The Things Left Behind

For your final writing piece of the semester, I am asking you to explore what is left behind. We discussed things left behind by the dead, what we inherit, manage, and decide to keep from those who leave us behind. We have spent time this unit looking at what we consider trash and why. The definition of waste expands from what we expel from our bodies to what is left as evidence of daily living. Finally, we discussed how we repurpose things in our own lives, what we keep that might otherwise be trashed or donated, how we use it and why.

Consider what the authors you have been reading have been doing in our readings. How can this help you write your own piece? Think about your peers' pieces and comments, what strikes you about their relationship to these objects? What from these themes inspires storytelling in you?

The essay should be about four to six pages, double-spaced in its final form. I encourage you to get this first draft as close to completion for our next class where we will do a formal peer review. You will also receive written feedback from me for revision. The more you get on the page, the more we can work with it!

Intention of the Assignment

This High Stakes assignment tends to be an opportunity for writers to engage in their most difficult reflection of the semester. What is left behind, whether it be trash or cherished items from family, holds a weight for most writers that the other objects don't. We work our way to this final assignment slowly throughout the semester because of the challenges inherent in the subject matter and the complexity of the range of topics to be considered.

Writers who have experienced loss of family and friends often take this as an opportunity to explore the meaning of that loss for themselves. Other writers take the opportunity to consider their own participation in the cycles of acquisition and purging. More often than not, this final essay tends to be the most serious in subject matter for all of my students. There is something about assessing cultural and personal values in relation to objects that are not intentionally acquired that makes us consider our own predilections as well as the societal messages around value that we have internalized. In this final project, we bring together all the lessons of the semester. There is a natural progression to this point of reflection, where we have the tools necessary to get to a deeper place in our writing. Together we consider the complex interactions we have with the objects left behind and what they reveal about how we value the relationships with stuff and people in our lives.

Student Example Essay #3—The Things Left Behind

Maximiliano De Paz—To Margarita

I'd like to think I've never experienced death in life before, but I have. When I was 7 years old, I lost my godmother. She was a caring older lady who took care of my cousin and I as kids. She introduced me to movies on VHS, video gaming, and helped me discover my everlasting rivalry with my cousin. Though vivid memories are so far in between when attempting to reminisce on events from 12 years ago, I do remember the week we lost her. It all felt so sudden; almost as if I didn't understand the magnitude of what was happening. I knew my parents, uncles, and cousins were crying, but I didn't feel anything remotely close to that. We went to her funeral service the next Saturday, but still, everything was okay to me. Maybe I couldn't read the room, but it was more likely that I didn't understand the concept of death. I still don't, but I do know that the objects that were left behind by my godmother allowed me to sink in the idea that death is real.

A few years after she passed, my godmother's husband decided to give away some of her possessions and my family was given the opportunity to take most of whatever we liked. It felt slightly strange and eerie, to be scavenging through the possessions of someone who no longer lives. It felt like exploring something that was just abandoned and left to sit in silence forever. In hindsight, I discovered an eclectic selection of objects that I decided to take into my possession. Some are physical, some are technological, others materialistic, but they've all helped me in further understanding what it means to lose someone in your life. Through these items, I hope to close off one of my childhood traumas and repurpose a loss from the past for a better future someday. Though a person may be lost forever, their possessions still live and with that, so does their presence.

The first item that I decided to keep for myself was an essential item from my past. It was an original Sega Genesis game console. Growing up, most of my free days when I wasn't at school were spent at my godmother's house with my cousin Sebastian as we played the Genesis. Our favorite game to play together was Sonic the Hedgehog. We weren't really good at the game and usually ended up smacking each other with the plastic controllers out of anger, but we played it during every visit. When I found it on the table of items being given away, I took a double glance before realizing what it was. It was dusty, scratched, and looked like a piece of junk, but I couldn't let its memory end up in a dumpster and eventually landfill. I decided to inherit the Genesis and I became rightful owner of it in that moment. I wasn't even sure if it worked still, but I decided to take on the opportunity regardless of its condition. Originally, I just had it on display on a shelf in my room but after some time, my curiosity continued to grow on whether or not it still worked. I decided to take a chance and got in contact with Sebastian, and we made it a mission to bring the Sega Genesis back to life.

Over the course of a week, we scavenged and assembled the missing parts of the console which included a pair of working controllers, an HDMI adapter to run on a modern flatscreen TV, and of course, a copy of *Sonic the Hedgehog*. By the end of the week, we gathered everything that was needed, and it was finally time to take the console off my shelf and into the living room. We dusted it off and did our tradition of blowing into the cartridge for good luck, before plugging in the controllers and cables. What ensued was the longest bit of silence I've ever experienced. The TV went pitch-black for about 20 seconds before a loud "SEGAAA" rang from the TV speakers followed by the legendary *Green Hill Zone* Sonic music. Sebastian and I jumped off the couch from excitement and thrill from bringing the Genesis back to life.

In that very moment, it felt as if my cousin and I were back in 2010 in my godmother's house playing the Sega while she served us our bowls of strawberries. In that moment, it felt as if there were no worries in the world again besides getting past the third level of *Sonic the Hedgehog*. We beat the game in a single sitting; something we were never able to do when we were younger, and we did it without beating the breaks off each other. What was a moment of taking the chance became a moment of fulfillment for my cousin and me. We both lost someone important to us in our lives at a young age and it was only years later that we were fully able to understand the magnitude of what we went through. Though we have grown further apart from each other as the years have passed, I am glad we were able to reunite like a tale of the past and close a difficult chapter from our lives. That's my brother forever. Through our revival of the Sega Genesis, we honored my godmother's memory and recollected on her presence. I put the Genesis back in my room, on the shelf where it continues to collect dust once again, but I carry its importance in every step of life that I take.

The second item(s) that I decided to inherit from my godmother are a collection of movies on VHS. For those unfamiliar (or uncultured), VHS was the dominant home media format for films before DVD's. My godmother raised me on her collection of VHS library. She had it all from *Jurassic Park* to Disney animated movies to Tarantino. She molded my love for not only the cinema, but for physical media and is a passion I have continued to carry with me throughout my life. I could've been greedy and taken the whole collection back home, but I decided to take the most important collection of movies to me which had to be the boxset of the original *Star Wars* trilogy. Some of my first memories in life were sitting in my godmother's living room watching *The Empire Strikes Back* with the sound and smell of instant popcorn lingering in the background. Sadly, I believe that we rewound the tape way too much when I was younger that they are no longer able to be played, but I think that's the bit of beauty in things that have been left behind. Sometimes, they just don't hold the value or purpose they once did and that's okay. Though the tapes are no longer playable, they sit in my room as a form of decoration. Nothing created is meant to last forever, both material and in life. Maybe it is trash to another person, but this is my gold. I could probably buy the same boxset from eBay, but it would hold no significance or connection to my life. It would just be a copy of the Star Wars movies and nothing more. But my boxset is meaningful to me because it comes from someone important from my past who no longer lives. Perhaps next time, in another life, I will meet her again and I can show her what she meant to me, but for now, this is all that is left of her in my life and all I can do for now is value them for what they are.

Though the items from my godmother hold minimal very little monetary worth, the memories, stories, and people attached make my inherited objects invaluable. When I stare at the high shelf in my room where the Sega Genesis and VHS tapes sit, I can't help but feel an abundance of emotions; whether that's sadness because my godmother never got to see my cousin and I grow up, or longing for life to be as it once was, but also comfort when realizing that my godmother is still with me even if it isn't physically. What was once hers is now mine and I intend to keep them and protect them just as she protected my younger self.

What was once an open and gushing untreated wound from childhood has now turned into a full circle moment has become a significant part of my transition in life from boy to man. Although the objects no longer work as they once did, they now serve a purpose beyond their original intention. They are so much more than objects from my past, but a remembrance of my late godmother, Margarita.

CONCLUSION

The Value of Assessing Our Relationships to Things

At the end of our classes together, my students often express gratitude for their new perspectives on the objects in their lives. They also share a palpable sense of frustration. Once we see things, we can't unsee them. Especially living in the busy and information-filled worlds we inhabit, we can become accustomed to tuning out so much of what surrounds us for expediency and survival. A shop goes out of business, we've passed it a hundred times, it's gone but what was there? We can't remember. We try to ignore those asking for help; we balk at tourists. You don't look up because it signals we are not from here. We pretend everyone can't see us when our blinds are up to let in the light or we have the most private conversations in public because we lack private space. We rarely enter friends' apartments in favor of meeting elsewhere because there is too much stuff in there and not enough room. In a city where we block so much out to survive, it can be a curse to be asked to notice.

Many of my students are involved in producing the very objects we are discussing. What does it mean to be part of this cycle of making stuff? This may not be your situation, but we are all part of the process of holding and consuming things. The implications can be heavy and burdensome, but reflecting on them in our writing can teach us and others a lot.

It can be a happy process to begin thinking about the objects in our lives, but we can become frustrated by analyzing them as well. Welcome to the conflicting emotions we all feel. We love our cherished objects, the smell of books, gifts from family and friends, beautiful art, and cozy cute clothing. Looking at the collections from childhood, the garbage we create, thinking about how we grew up, familial attitudes, cultural codes, the push to consumerism from social media, the pull of sustainability, and personal responsibility for the future of our planet, and what it is about stuff that they enjoy can bring up complex and even conflicting emotions. Thinking about stuff is fun, exciting, and exhausting. Sometimes we just want to have objects out of sight, want something new, want to donate and throw things away, or want to admire and aspire to be a better person with better stuff.

This book in no way can provide a comprehensive overview of all the topics broached. Each idea is worthy of further reading and study. You may find that certain concepts speak to you more than others. I encourage you to keep reading to continue deepening your understanding of the subjects here and explore what others have written about them. What I find fascinating about this object inquiry is that it doesn't seem to have any bounds; it can lead to so many new ideas and paths for writing. My hope is you will find inspiration here and explore beyond the limited examples I have been able to provide.

What is the value of assessing these objects in our lives? Perhaps beyond reflecting on our own material reality and relationship to the world, it could be little. We might be able to craft a story that preserves and helps us to understand a family history and tie to things we keep. We might be able to change our view of what we surround ourselves with and our relationship to others that manifests because of it. We may simply enjoy the journey of exploring and coming to know ourselves and our passions through our things and the things of others. It can push us to consider our work and what we produce as a result of it. There is something about the tangibility of objects that compels us all to want to touch, own, admire, toss, and explore them.

How to Keep Engaging Object Writing Beyond This Book

As I said from the beginning, this book is not a comprehensive look at the world of objects; it is only the tip of the iceberg. I hope this exploration has helped you to notice, consider, and write about the things you may cherish as much as the things you may overlook.

As I mention throughout the book, I encourage writers to enter their local communities and consider these lessons in their personal lives. Your writing may be for a class or yourself, but your writing could also become part of the larger conversation through publishing or just discussing the importance of things that have been otherwise overlooked with others. Visit local institutions, offices, libraries, museums, and archives. Venture out to recycling centers and garbage treatment facilities. Talk to your friends and family members about what they collect and value and why. Take a look at what you surround yourself with and what you discard and consider its value to you.

In my teaching, I always remind students that writing itself is an important act. We never know how our words will impact the larger world, and that is scary and exciting. I am impressed with the work my students have done that has extended into the larger conversations of their creative output, their communities, their family lives, and their efforts toward sustainability. This is why I have included so many of their wonderful and thought-provoking pieces in this book. Thinking in order to write about stuff can show us the importance of what surrounds us and how we can deepen our understanding of the complicated worlds in which we live. I hope you can all add your writing on things to the writings found here.

Recently on a trip to Lake Superior, I began to notice the rocks on the shore as my spouse and son tried their hand at fishing. I had never thought about the rocks underfoot before, mostly finding them burdensome to walk and sit on. But I was bored and I started looking more closely. Some of these rocks were shiny and had deep veins through them. Some were pockmarked and had little holes that contained crystals. I began to pick up and admire the rocks; they were beautiful. I found out something many people already knew: that the shores of the Great Lakes are covered in agates. People congregate online to share their finds. Books have been written on how to identify your stones and people teach classes on how to be a successful rock hound. This all came from a moment of boredom and looking—the objects underfoot revealed a whole complex world I never knew about.

Personal Memoir

This piece was the original conclusion to my memoir about growing up in the antiques business. It reflects how my early life came to influence my current life with objects. I will leave you with this piece of my own personal writing in hopes that it inspires you to keep considering how the themes we have explored throughout this book continue to be a source of inspiration for your writing journey ahead.

There is a calm in the morning—waking up with the pain of leaving the warmth of my bed before I begin to drive and before the sun has even considered rising. I am 17 and needing sleep desperately as only a teenager can. I navigate by the clearest brightest stars and the essence of sleeping woods while the whir of the truckers steadily hums past the breathing warmth of my car on the highway. I doze and coast along the lanes, letting myself linger in my haze, knowing my car will find its way. It's the same kind of calm that will allow my car to crash into a telephone pole at a full 45 miles per hour, cracking my sternum a year later. Deer peek out of roadside trees with eyes that, like the street signs overhead, pop with the flash of my headlights. I can smell the dust of the objects in my backseat and trunk—a mustiness from their various cycles through the damp mornings at the markets, where dew forms on books and drips down glass and the chill of the dark penetrates my layers straight into my bones.

The gravel crunches as I pull into the lot and crickets tweet outside my car window. I settle in under a large familiar oak tree that will protect me from the midday sun. Last year, right in front of my table, one of its large limbs came crashing down at noon, decapitating a dealer—a story is born. I return to it like a second home and turn off my engine to sit, to wait. It will be hours before the light comes. I curl up in my front seat listening to the radio voices of construction workers calling in to find comfort in the fact that others are awake too. Sipping on a coffee, dozing slightly, cars come pulling into their spots. Jacketed dealers saunter out, adjusting their tables just so according to their own rituals. They place heavy metal objects on top, rocks, clear enough space to walk in between, push them close enough to prevent others from doing the same. Spreading sheets, cloths, newspapers to stake a claim on what is rightfully theirs, trying desperately to justify the early commute.

As I hide and listen to my radio on low, people emerge one by one and start moving around the market like gently stirring molecules. Customers pop up and begin to walk aimlessly in the dark, searching but not knowing for what, bouncing off tables, appearing and disappearing under dim streetlights that illuminate the aisles. Sellers begin to buzz, begin small conversations, avoid unpacking, wait for the men with flashlights to come around, shining them in cars, front seats, trunks undercover, looking suspiciously, expectantly at stacks of boxes, asking fervent questions, hoping to get a positive response to just one of them from someone, anyone. Got any jewelry? Coins? Toys? Any dolls today? Guitars? Later in the day others will come looking for keys, boy scout memorabilia, cameras—unlike the early eager vultures, the late morning guys have a consistent calm gimmick, an identity they show in their clothes and the way they ask questions without expecting answers. They wear vests of patches, advertising their goods on their hats, noticeable as much for the time they come as what they carry, doing the rounds day after day week after week at different markets, friendly familiar strangers looking more for companionship than merchandise, when you have what they want, lacking the money to buy it. I have many friends of this ilk that collect around my table during the day, broken gold guy, record collector, and amateur photography connoisseur none of whom ever buy anything from me. They tease me about my merchandise—it is old, dirty, unpriced. They tell me the same stories over and over again and I share parts of my life with them. They know me from the time I am six years old and every year I tell them something new—I am in school, living abroad, teaching, a doctor. I change while they stay the same, telling me the same stories, smiling just as quizzically as I tell them mine.

"Any Ummmmm", "I think so, let me check". They get excited. In the early morning before the sunrise it is all in the timing, the slow reveal. It is a burlesque show, a tease, contingent on the excitement you can create for the flashlights. You can't put all your goods on the table right away, it's not exciting. It's stale. There's no anticipation, no chase. You have to wait, unpack slowly, hook them with something good, an eye catcher, a guitar, something flashy, cut glass vase, something not too expensive, just expensive enough, large enough, tempting enough, weird enough. Antique fishing rods. A crossbow. Abstract painting. Hook them, get them excited about what more they might get to see, what's inside your boxes, under the sheets, in the car. Reserve a few things and pull them out when they ask for them. It came from grandma's attic, my old neighbor's basement, an auction in the country. You have to slowly tease, pull out, carefully unwrap fresh merchandise, and stuff you haven't been able to unload for weeks, alternate. The bad looks good when it's placed right, adjusted just so, in the midst of beauty. If you've got great tits, they won't notice the scar on your navel. Convince them as you distract them with your pasties that old merchandise is new.

I never ever price anything, instead, I read the customers. After I catch their interest, I hook them with numbers. Numbers come out in batches depending on who it is and how I feel, ringing out low enough to get interest from them and the others hovering nearby. The more they buy the more expensive it gets cause when you start low there is an expectation—I am giving it away, I don't know what it's worth, I am underselling, desperate, young, pretty, dumb. They may know me for twenty years, but the buyers are dying to be convinced and my cool demeanor convinces them. Like my grandmother, I wake early, take a shower, apply make-up, do my hair, I am attractive, young, composed, well rested and they smell it on me. Always. They are putting one over on me, they know better than me, this time, they've got me. I sell things cheap, really cheap, less than they are worth to start, just like a drug dealer—this is how I get them hooked. They will make stacks, pay anything without question, and as they feed, others feed. No time to pause or think, or the others will go for it. They pile. The feeding frenzy, I have to catch it and maintain it for as long as I can. The slow reveal and then I let it all fly, I talk, I never make eye contact. Concentrate on my unpacking as they pile up, push, drool, grab, grab, grab as the numbers quickly fly off my tongue 5, 30, 100, 10, 7, 7, 7—I'm in a 7 mood. Others buy things they don't want, it's so cheap maybe they can get a piece. I take their piles of cash, don't even bother to count it, shove the pile in my pocket with the other piles, thank them, flash a huge smile, move on to the next who is just waiting to give me all they've got. I don't care; money is nothing to me. Merchandise is nothing to me. There will be plenty of time for counting later. The bills pile, I run out of grocery bags, I clear half my merchandise in 20 minutes and then it is over—they are gone and the sun has somehow risen. I step more slowly now, and arrange, rotate, clean up, check the piles in my pockets are still there—I have a long morning ahead of me. No rush. I take my time. I am naked. It is 6:00 a.m and time for a new cup of coffee. I sneak into the front seat of the car and close the door. I unfold the crumpled bills, carefully arranging them in a neat stack. $447, I will most likely make only another $50 over the next six hours. I settle in. People ask after my grandmother, carefully, nervously, is she still doing the market? It is Wednesday, the cheap day where I pay only $5 for my two tables; Grandma and Maggie do the market on Sundays, which requires reservations and $40. "Of course," I reply. "Kicking and strong."

"How old is she now?"

"86, 89, 92 . . ." it never ends, until it does.

My grandma in the last year and a half or her life when she can no longer do the market tells me every morning she wakes up, she feels like she's sixteen, until she looks in the mirror and says, "Who is this old bag?" I continue on for her.

ADDITIONAL STUDENT EXAMPLES

Assignment #1 (Informal "Low Stakes")—Bedroom Objects

David Lapointe—Digital Camera

Over the past 5 years I've been subconsciously in review documenting my life experiences and sometimes lessons through the objects I've acquired through life, most of which come from a very specific time in my childhood. I write quite often to three objects, some more than others, all evoking emotions that are completely different from one another.

The object I would like to talk about today is a digital camera that my mother gave me in 2006. We brought that digital camera everywhere. We brought it to our beach days after school, garage parties with my Portuguese grandparents, for selfies with my mom and her Blackberry, photos of her sponge painted bedroom and so much more. It was our way to document our relationship.

This object holds so much meaning to me because It no longer works but I still have the SD card that holds all those memories that I think of on a daily basis. We used to live in an apartment that overlooked a baseball field and every night we would have the concession stand throw peanuts up at us and eat them while sitting in the kitchen sink. One day my mom pulled out the camera and snaps a photo of me pointing to a shooting star. She said, "you can make a wish or you can write what you want to say to yourself in your 20s and put it in this glass bottle." The glass bottle, another piece I often write to.

My life completely changed almost instantaneously from that day. My mom developed ovarian cancer and fell really sick and so much more we can explore later in this semester. I still tear up about this camera because it documented all the things that were beautiful in my life just up until the moments they got ugly. I always think that this camera died for a reason and that was to leave what happened after up to me—do I let the ugly moments define who I am or aid in what I learn? I still write to that exact moment the shutter of the camera went off, what did I wish for? What would I have told myself in my twenties? Am I still the same or am I unrecognizable? I cherish this camera because it ties me back to a time that otherwise I feel without would feel much fuzzier.

Assignment #2 (Informal "Low Stakes")—Collecting

Hailey Duffett—Collection

Male deer, bucks, shed their antlers around when the new year rolls around. Each year these bones fall to the ground and other animals gobble them up for nutrients and a meal. That is unless my dad or "shed collectors" like him, come and find the antlers first. My dad is a hunter, he grew up in Virginia, and took up the hobby when he was young. Although I know there is something to say about putting in the work at something and later reaping the reward, my mom and I often talk about how he likes to hunt just so that he can sit alone away from us for a while. So when about four years ago my dad had a new micro obsession pop up overnight, my mom and I agreed that it followed his introverted tendencies to just be alone and have something to show for it at the end of the day.

My dad goes on "walks" as he calls them. However, they are actually well planned, tracked, photographed, and driven searches for deer antlers that often last over 10 miles in the woods. Over the past four years my dad has collected over a hundred deer antlers. In fact, when calling him on the phone to just ask some basic questions about his collection, within seconds he listed off the exact number of antlers per year that was added.

When I am enjoying my Christmas vacation and sleeping in much too late, my dad will wake up after doing extensive research on google maps of parks nearby and set out. He has even traveled as far as 2 hours away to just get to a park that has "ideal deer conditions". Once at the park he starts an app on his phone called "onyx" which tracks where he walks and he can add photos of landmarks and found antlers. Once he sees one, before even picking it up off of the ground, he takes pictures of it untouched. After he is home, he prints out the pictures, labels them with the date and number of deer antler per year, and puts them into a binder. In this binder you can also find a printed out excel spreadsheet that includes information on each antler, including the color, interesting titles I don't understand, a description of any markers on the antlers, and even the GPS coordinates of where they were found. Over 3 inches thick with reprints of all of his photos, and the spreadsheet with all of this very valuable information, you can imagine the tragedy that ensued when my mom spilled a glass of wine on it over the summer, because yes, of course the binder is displayed on the coffee table year-round.

This all may seem very foreign to any other family than my own. But to me, I have heard extensive information on the ideal conditions to look for deer antlers, how their trails interact, how they are likely to be by fences (falling off from the jump), and even how a deer can be tracked over the years through the increase in spikes on the antlers and length showing the growth of the deer. My dad is honestly meticulous. Our living room has baskets full of these found antlers. Walking into my house you couldn't avoid seeing them if you tried. My dad thinks that they are some kind of home decor, but my mom and I agree that they have definitely become a little out of control, being strewn about on the furniture. That being said, when assigned this prompt, I immediately thought of my dad and all of his antlers. He takes pride in every single one and really enjoys looking for them. So at the end of the day, he is happy, and I have a story to tell for this essay. At home there are deer antlers and thinking of them now makes me happy. I love my dad and he loves collecting deer antlers. I honestly think it is as simple as that.

Essay #1 (Formal "High Stakes" Assignment)—Collections

Justin Murphy—Be a Good "Boy"

It was tradition when I went to my cousin's house to play my favorite game, "Justina". My two cousins would spend hours painting my nails, putting on my makeup, and styling me in the most extravagant *Justice* store attire they owned. Luckily for me I had not hit puberty yet, so the body was looking snatched. I would go parading through the halls as I felt the fantasy of being a girl. My Aunt would smile and laugh right alongside the girls who made such a beauty. One day while the glam team was getting me together for my big reveal, their neighbor decided to stop by. As my eyes were being coated with the deepest blue shade of their five-dollar makeup kit, I heard footsteps approaching my so-called dressing room. He looked at me and uttered a word I had never heard before. That was the first time I got called a faggot; I was nine.

Today, twenty-one years old, my makeup routine is muscle memory. It is an intricate fourteen step process that usually takes me an hour to do. It's so easy now, freeing even. When I'm alone in my room, pounding my foundation into my skin with my beauty blender, I feel like me. It wasn't always like that. For someone like me, I had to fight for this complex step-by-step routine. So many people are ignorant to the fact that wearing makeup is a privilege. Someone doing the same thing I am hasn't been spit on, called a freak, chased out of the 6 train while strangers watched, laughed at, and constantly told they are doing something wrong. These "bullies" real issue is my queerness, but that's for a bigger conversation unrelated to my makeup skills. My journey of being able to walk in a room as the confident gender queer person I am now, started somewhere ironically, with the help of five foundations I still have today.

Mom's It Cosmetic BB Cream

I had a two-hour window from when I got home from school until my mom would get home. In those two hours, I would go into my mom's makeup bag and smear her bb cream, which she still thinks is equivalent to foundation, all over my face. It was about two shades too orange and would completely drip down my fingers to the palms of my hands making it seem I used a bad fake tanner. I had so much product to apply and not enough time. Tick Tick Tick. Each product I put on my acne-engulfed face was like a snooze button on my alarm clock; each time I hit snooze I knew that the final alarm would soon be going off. As 5:00 approached my heart would sink and my anxiety would kick in. I had twenty minutes to look like the "good boy" my mom raised. In a blink of an eye my clothes were off and I was in the shower; it would happen so fast that the water never had time to heat up. I would scrub my face so hard that there was not a trace of makeup left. A part of me would rub so hard to wipe away the shame of wanting to wear makeup in the first place. I was so sick and tired of this daily ritual. I knew I couldn't keep using my mom's makeup. She is going to find out that someone's been stealing her makeup when the tube becomes empty, and well, I'm the only one in the house, so unless we have a secret live-in guest, all fingers point to me. She will find out that I'm not normal. I needed my own supplies to perfect my craft.

E.L.F. Cosmetics Flawless Satin Foundation

The lights were so bright and it smelt like the entire place was coated in Fabuloso. It definitely was to hide the musky smell of a fast-paced shopping mall. I was on high alert, making sure no one I knew was in the store before I entered and continuously was checking around to make sure no one came in after me. I didn't even know what I was looking for. A worker approached, "Hello welcome to E.L.F. Do you need any help today?" My insides were turning upside down. I didn't know what to say or what to ask for. I also didn't know if I wanted their help; I was still so ashamed I was in a makeup store. "Um, I'm looking for makeup," I uttered. Like wow no shit girl, how stupid I kept saying in my head. Thankfully for me, the worker smiled and went to work. She made me a little basket with the essentials. As I got home and ran to my room I was pleased to find my new foundation. It was pretty good and lasted me three whole months, but it was on to the next.

Makeup Forever Stick Foundation

My junior year of high school the YouTube makeup community was in full throttle. Everywhere you looked a new makeup trend was being created by one of the top makeup influencers. My favorites were James Charles, Jeffree Star, and Jaclyn Hill. Whatever makeup hack or new product came out that they used I had to have. I would save up all my money from my part-time retail job to get the most high-end palettes, brushes, lipsticks and of course, foundation. At the time, James Charles raved about the Makeup Forever Stick Foundation. So, of course I had to go and get it. I think I truly believed that if I used the products that these big talented influencers used I would somehow gain all the makeup skills that they had. Back to the mall I went to get the Makeup Forever Stick Foundation in the shade "sand." I knew my mom was going to be home since it was a

Sunday, her only day off. The packaging was so small I could have easily stuck it in my pocket, but for a cross-dressing teen, that thought didn't cross my mind. As my friend's mom pulled up to my driveway to drop me off I scavenged through the backseat of the car in hopes to find a bag from a store that screamed "MOM I AM A HETEROSEXUAL" on it. As I looked under the passenger seat I found a tiny GameStop bag. That could work; I think, straight people play video games, as I begged my friend to let me have it. I didn't really beg, it was more like, "My mom can't see this Sephora bag because she'll know her son's a fag, can I have this bag so she thinks I'm blowing up zombies in a video game?," but begging sounded more dramatic. As I shove the foundation stick into the bag, I felt relieved. I said thank you to my friend's mom and walked inside. My mom was asleep on the couch.

Tarte Cosmetics Born This Way Foundation

It was my best friend's mom's wedding. For weeks I would talk about how I am going to do full glam to the reception. I was excited to show off my new skills to the hundreds of strangers that were going to be there. I was finally comfortable wearing makeup in public and all my friends were great; teaching me more about my new found passion. The day has finally come, and I began starting the beat. As I opened the packaging to my new foundation I knew what had to be done. An hour and a half later the look was complete with a purple cut crease that matched my button up I planned on wearing. I was so happy. "Are you ready yet?" my mom said as she opened up the door. I will never forget the way that my mom looked at me that day. Her eyes became dark and her body began to actually cringe. "What is that, why are you wearing that?" she said on the verge of tears. I didn't really plan for my mom's reaction. I've been wearing makeup for almost two years at this point that I forgot that my mom had no idea. My heart started to beat faster and faster as I thought of something to say. "It's makeup," I whispered. I could feel her disappointment as I said it. All the feelings I had as a kid that I was somehow doing something wrong came back like a tsunami storming a village. "No! No, get it off right now! You can't be wearing that. Boys don't wear makeup. What's wrong with you?," she shouted. There, there it is, what's wrong with me, as if my existence is incorrect. I was in so much shock that I didn't know what to do or say. I felt paralyzed. I grabbed my makeup wipes and began rubbing my face. She watched me in my doorway rubbing away a mix of tears and makeup.

The car ride to the wedding was silent. It took three years for that silence to be broken.

HourGlass Soft Glow Foundation

My final foundation. For the past six months this has been the dewy liquid that I apply to my face. It hides my acne scars, but still gives a more natural look. It can be seen at family parties, nights out in New York City, and if I get up early enough, this classroom. It is the foundation that gives me my armor to this ugly word we are living in. Being a non-binary person, looking in the mirror can be challenging sometimes; all I see is a man. Even when I put on pounds of makeup, the most expensive human hair wig, the highest heel, the world sees me as a man. I have been struggling recently with this. I will be literally in a wig and someone will still say "he." I honestly think it is the most bullshit excuse when people will say "they" is an adjustment and continue to say "he." When I went from Justin to my nickname Murph, there was no stumble, mistakes, or hesitations. Why does saying "they" create such a challenge for people? With all the recent anti-trans legislation it feels hopeless; like the world will never see me. I know trans men and women have it harder than me, especially those of color, but for gender non-conforming people who may look like the sex they were assigned at birth it can feel defeating when the world just doesn't get it. However, I love myself too much to bring my joy down. I wake up every day happy to be alive in a body that I know is mine; that is capable of loving freely and deeply. This foundation helps me have gender euphoria due to its full coverage of my manly face features. It makes me feel seen and I hope that others can understand their authenticity the way that I have.

Renée Dery—Hair Dye

At this current moment, I have 11 bottles of hair dye scattered around my bedroom. Three of which are half empty, left from previous hair colors that I've taken on over the past year. Pathways to three old versions of myself, and the rest collected as options for future eras. I change my hair as the seasons change as signs that I'm not staying stagnant. With the power of a bucket of bleach and a bottle of pigment, I hold all of the power in my transformation. I can use the dye to forcefully turn over a new leaf and start a new chapter in which I'm better than ever before.

I tell myself I don't get rid of them in case I ever need them again. But I think that realistically, I just use them to remind myself how far I've come.

I've always used my hair as a method to define who I am. My hair is brown, naturally curly, and very thick. When I was young it held a lot of depth and shine, courtesy of all of the time I spent in the sun which helped to lighten it. I remember once my dad's work partner told me that women paid to have hair like mine. I held that compliment with me for a very long time, so I let it grow. I let it grow and grow, until it was the longest out of the girls in my class, and until I was mostly known for my thick, brown mane. I always wore my hair down because I thought I looked bad in ponytails; they made my face far too visible.

I started sweating a lot in middle school. Puberty mixed with the boatload of anxiety that I'd been carrying with me since preschool. My hair helped to cover my sweat stains and I cried when my parents forced me to cut four inches from it in the 7th grade. I started to straighten it to make it easier to manage and also because I was just about the only girl left who didn't straighten her hair. I started high school with hair down to my butt, which I would never dare let go behind my ears. I wanted it to cover as much of me as possible.

I cut eleven inches from my hair at the end of my freshman year, quite the literal weight taken off of my shoulders. My thick hair was now light enough to curl up, connecting me back to how I knew it as a child. I began paying more attention to the way that I dressed, as it was no longer going to be completely covered by my hair. I got highlights for the first time about six months after that, my first adventure into dye, but you would barely be able to tell. Subtlety was my way of survival in those times. I wouldn't have risked doing anything super drastic because that might draw attention to me. I had never gotten large amounts of attention before, so I wouldn't know how to handle it if I did.

I had an appointment to go blonde one week after the world shut down due to the pandemic, a very horrible period of time, which unfortunately probably saved my life and made me who I am today. I feel weird and a little guilty about that, but the isolation forced me to unearth my queerness, which has fundamentally altered my place in the world. Also, it was the first time that I used box hair dye. Target delivery helped remedy my cancelled hair appointment blues, and I dyed the underside of my hair pink, the first time that color made its way into my hair. At that point in time, I had just begun identifying as bisexual, which makes the half covered and temporary aspect of that hair color feel quite fitting.

I kicked off my senior year of high school with my blonde dreams, which was the most drastic hair change I had experienced. I don't always have the best reactions to change, but to my surprise, it made me feel more confident. My realizations from the previous summer meant that I now aimed to stand out instead of fading into obscurity. It was with this hair color that I applied to FIT, began thrift shopping, and gained a new established reputation as "cool girl". It felt good to finally feel like people knew something about me besides my name. I look at my blonde era as the final steppingstone. After that I was ready to take the next step back into color, and I booked a hair appointment for that winter break.

That winter break I fell really hard for one of my best friends, and to my luck and surprise the feeling was mutual. We began dating on December 27, 2020, and five days later I dyed my hair bright green. It was in the same week that I realized I was a lesbian. I can't separate the memory of the three events no matter how hard I try. Discovering I was a lesbian felt like a rebirth, and my colored hair felt like I was finally embodying who I had always been deep down. Having dyed hair became a signifier of my lesbian identity, and the memory of my bright green hair became linked with my first girlfriend.

I usually think about this time as "The Hayden Era", because the duration of that hair color is roughly the same as the duration of our relationship. I feel very bittersweet about those five months. On the one hand I had finally felt like a complete person for the first time. I was accessing a range of emotions I had never known were there. But, it's also quite hard to be in a secret relationship with a closeted girl, when all I really wanted to do was display to the world how proudly queer I was. My girlfriend loved my hair, she still cites it as her favorite hair color of mine. But I was now one of the queerest people at Commack High School, so being seen with me was a risk to her. She's right, it looked very good, and it made people think about me in a different way.

The complicated emotional ties I have to that era meant that hair color had to be retired for good. That relationship taught me a lot about who I am. The first time experiencing romantic feelings is much more transformative than I can put into words. It forced me to change the way that I perceived myself, and the way others interacted with me. I spent that era confused, and I'm not sure if I'll ever want to see myself like that again.

I dyed my hair blue about two weeks after Hayden broke up with me, a color I pre-planned to match my prom dress, but the shift in appearance after a breakup was very welcome. I attended the dance with my three best friends, and that summer the four of us became completely inseparable. Still recovering from my first lesbian heartbreak, and freshly graduated from high school, I came out publicly online. I started learning who I was as a lesbian who wasn't in a relationship. I surrounded myself with queer joy that came from my friendships and let myself act stupid for the first time in my life. It was a chaotic and dramatic summer, and I cried violently while saying goodbye to my best friends as we departed for college. And of course, I dyed my hair.

Orange was the next color up. A controversial pick, considering the fact that my ex, who I was very much not over yet, was a ginger. I'm still debating about whether the two are connected, but I loved it nonetheless. This was my fall of freshman year hair, a semester that ended up being drama-filled and complicated. I did love my first semester at FIT, because I knew deep down that I belonged there. However, thinking back on that time tends to make me sad, because I know the girl with the orange hair is going through it. The switch to magenta hair meant that I started my spring semester. After a difficult fall, I became determined to ditch the drama and focus on handling myself better. A new hair color meant that I had a clean slate to do this. I took 21 credits that semester, which proved to be a lot of work, but I had finally settled down and began to feel more confident in my future and my past. I grew a lot during this first year, and so I decided to shave my head.

People tend to associate shaving one's head with mental breakdowns, but I felt quite the opposite. This decision, as with all of my hair decisions, was highly thought out. As we can all tell, I care deeply about my hair. My crazy colors are not a sign of impulsivity, but months of careful deliberation about who I want to be. When I shaved my head, it meant that I had healed. It meant that I no longer felt as though I needed to hide behind my hair to prevent others from looking at me. I no longer needed to dim my queerness for the benefit of another person. My hair still held all the memories of my anxious, insecure, and heartbroken self. I needed to rid myself of my hair in order to let go of those feelings. So, I don't feel pity for the girl with the crewcut, I feel proud that she made it so far.

That was 16 months ago, and since then I've cycled through four different hair colors and a variety of different cuts as I let it grow out. I started dying it myself, because I realized that no one else is going to execute my visions the way I want them to. And that's how I started collecting hair dye. I take comfort in the fact that I have eight unopened bottles of dye, as it means I have access to new pathways. Eight different options in a "choose your own adventure" that will help to define the next season of my life. Dying my hair myself means that I have control over the future versions of myself. It means that I have access to a clean slate whenever my current season has run its course.

I feel like so much more of a real person when my hair is freshly dyed and interesting. My next color is something that I've thought about ever since the last time I dyed it. The feeling of a new color is something that I've grown to crave. Maybe it's the 5+ years of therapy that has forced me to embrace change, or maybe it's the fact that I spent the first 14 years of my life trying to maintain consistency. But for me, change can't just happen on the inside, because how else am I supposed to prove to the world that I'm different than I was. So, I won't be throwing out my old hair dye, even though I have nowhere to store it. It feels like it's grown to be a part of who I am, and moving on would feel like I'm leaving parts of me behind. Remnants from all of the people who I used to be, and keys to all of the people who I have yet to become.

Cassandra Hughes—An Anthology of Accumulation

May 9, 2022, "It's October now and I can't remember most things of my life and my brain can't retain everything I've ever witnessed. There are pictures and little scribbles I drew in preschool and everything I have obsessively tried to capture since. My phone is running out of picture storage and I'm not sure how much longer I can save every single birthday card I've ever been gifted . . ."

I've never had a good memory. I find comfort knowing all those who I no longer speak to are receding into depths of my memory I can't quite reach now. The good parts of my life are receding as well. To collect is to preserve, it is to remember. When I look around my bedroom and question the reason and meaning of the idea of collection, everything makes sense aesthetically. I like pinks, greens, and rich jewel tones. I gravitate towards gaudy jewelry, hatpins, trinket dishes and anything that happens to have cabochon stones. I like old books, illustration prints, ornate frames and planters. I've always been fond of Russian nesting dolls as I grew up around them. I like brass and gold, copper and wood, natural and rugged yet shiny and mystical. None of this is consistent in subject yet I know what I like and it all stems from an anecdote. Most of my jewelry belonged to my mom, or my grandma, or somebody else's grandma. I love thinking about women who came before me, what were their lives like? How did they experience the world? It all comes back to being a woman, it all comes back to being a little girl. I bought a large gold frame once at a place called the junk shop near my town. I wanted to paint over the portrait inside to make a landscape for my bedroom walls. My mom made a comment that the woman in the portrait was probably someone's Grandma, probably passed now, and the work had been commissioned for their family. I painted over it anyways, the painting was mine to be fair. I regretted it immediately, and I felt as though I erased a woman's existence. Why was the painting sitting in that junk shop in the first place?

A collection is a portrait in a way. I think a photograph of myself could never encapsulate who I am, but an image of the top of my dresser probably could. Unless you write a book about yourself or you're loud enough that people tell your story for you, what you own is all that lives beyond you. Your family or loved ones can do that for you, or some teenage girl can find your favorite ring in a thrift shop 50 years after your death and love it too. It brings meaning back to objects, they're more than just objects. I can wear a cameo necklace that a woman wore before me hundreds of years ago. There's a shared story there in passing down objects through time. It's an attempt to feel connected to each other without really ever knowing one another.

Collection is preservation. Historically and personally I find myself drawn to memory, desperately scrambling to find mementos. I've never thrown out a birthday card, or a gift from an ex. I gravitate towards anything vintage, hints of the past. I write every day, how I'm feeling, what I did.

November 11, 2022 "there is something about churches at nighttime, I wish I could go to church again. To smell the pages of the hymn book on Sunday morning, wearing dusty white robes as I light the altar candles. I wish I knew who to pray to."

There is such a disconnect from myself and a younger version of me. That's probably why I'm searching every day for some sort of connection; there's a childish need to make a timeline. There was such a specific iconography of my childhood. Wet hair, dirty socks, dried flowers, chalk dust on my fingers. Her world was more colorful, she depended less on some false sense of escapism. That little girl exists outside of me and I just hope I find her. She collected rocks and shells and wore cowboy hats with pajamas and wrote in a locket diary before bedtime. Her favorite little stuffed animal was a giraffe that wore a nightcap; it recited her bedtime prayer with her when she held it close, *"Now I lay me down to sleep, I pray the Lord my soul to keep, and if I should die before I wake, I pray the Lord my soul to take."* That little girl wore an enameled butterfly charm around her neck and kept pennies in her pocket. She doesn't even know who she is yet, but she likes how she feels when she wears dresses and begs her mother to let her get her ears pierced. She glues rhinestones to her earlobes, mocking an image of women older and more beautiful. She gets her ears pierced when she's 11 years old and has a pair of earrings for each day of the week by 12.

December 4, 2021, "when I was five I would sit in the herb garden, feel the squishiness of crushing blackberries beneath my fingers. Mom is teaching me how to play chess, I have 7 cavities and my baby teeth are getting wobbly. Mom puts them in a pouch beneath my pillow when the dentist pulls them out, I hope they're gone when I wake up."

My family went to Cape Cod every August. When we were children, my dad would bring huge buckets each year and we'd collect seashells till we were sunburnt and our fingertips were pruney. I was a professional at catching the golden glint of the mermaids' toenails resting on the sand; they were always my favorite. When we got home from vacation my dad would soak them to get the smell out and then help me drill holes in them to wear as jewelry and adornments. It feels like I'm wearing my childhood when I put them on, like I could still be that young.

June 15, 2022, "I struggle with tangibility, I wish I could sit at your kitchen table one last time. Do you remember when I made you an anklet made of thin golden shells? I still have mine in a drawer I haven't opened in years. I hope you do too."

As a child I would sit on my Grandmother's living room floor, pulling apart the layers of her Russian Nesting Dolls. They had a new face and colors with each reveal. I was mesmerized by the intricacy of these wooden figurines. The symbolism of being able to have so much depth, to have so many identities under the surface. I believe I have always personified these dolls, I see myself in them. In high school I wrote a poem for a poetry class about my Grandma's dolls but it's not really about the dolls at all,

"We would lay on grandma's living room floor Girls and boys dirty after playing in the garden,
Now tearing apart the onion skin layers of Russian nesting dolls.
The most vivid shades of blue and green you had ever seen, the complexity diminishing with each doll.
I grew fond of the smallest doll.
She suffered no loss of color, she depended on the rest.
I soon became the smallest nesting doll, I would grow to wrap myself in other people.
I became accustomed to the belief that you are made of those present during your creation, made of those you coat yourself in.
I am a Russian nesting doll.
I make myself out of others . . ."

I find as I get older, I become more superstitious. I keep a cross in my pocket, I tie my shoelaces twice. I don't know if I believe in God, but I collect cross Jewelry and rosaries anyways. I was once just a little girl sitting in church pews as a source of comfort. All my Catholic family members keep crosses over each doorway in their home. I hung up one in my bedroom as well; it makes me feel like I fit in better. I don't pray anymore, but how could anything bad happen to me with a cross in my pocket and my mom's protective selenite bracelet on? Protection is very important to me these days. I never felt very unsafe as a child, that all changed when I moved to the city. Nothing truly bad has ever happened to me but I feel at ease with certain objects on me when I'm out and about. I have a cross in my pocket, a stone in my purse, selenite bracelet, Virgin Mary necklace on and a collection of hat pins in my purse. I started collecting hat pins for no particular reason, I just found them beautifully intricate and I felt the need to own them. I get most of them in large antique stores in Maine where my dad lives. I don't even wear hats but maybe I'll start as my collection grows. I learned recently that hatpins were popularly worn by women in New York City when women were first allowed to use the subway. These women on their daily commutes were often harassed by men and left with little to nothing to defend themselves; these women used their hatpins as weapons. I too as a woman in New York City 100 years later understand what these women must have felt at times, but nonetheless it's almost kind of comforting in a way to know maybe one of these hatpins I own could have put a shitty man in his place long before I was even born.

My collections go in phases, I find that when I reflect back on my life the object I fixated on collecting reflects my priorities and passions in that era. When I was 10, I started collecting postcards from everywhere I went. I loved to travel and I thought travel was the most important thing in life. I loved traveling so much that I believed that I was going to grow up and become a photojournalist. I aspired to jump from country to country with a camera and a notepad in some hyper glamorized and unrealistic ideals of what a journalist actually does. I obviously never become a journalist and I'm not working on it anymore either. Hopefully she would be proud of what I'm doing now, she didn't even know who she was yet. So many of these collections have ended up in boxes, how could I ever throw anything out when I place such importance on irrelevant objects? If I throw out the box of letters and gifts from my first boyfriend, did I ever even date him? I don't even remember what he looked like, so some scribbled notes from 15 years old is all I have for some sense of nostalgia if I ever decide to feel sentimental about that time of my life. I know hoarding has a negative connotation to it, but I'll admit that's the route I'm heading down. At 21 years old I already have an abundance of useless things. So much of it brings me joy, but maybe the entire spectrum of emotions these collections evoke is worthwhile as well. I wish I had everything I've ever owned, if only my closet was infinite I could archive my entire existence like some sort of museum exhibit.

May 6, 2022, "all things end in October, I too must acknowledge how to leave those parts of myself in boxes. I will never forget the month of October, it is where all things come from, I believe it is where all things end. I was born on October 26, 2001 and I feel as though I will never exist outside of that autumnal comfort."

Assignment #4 (Informal "Low Stakes")—Gendered Objects

Scott Krupa—Lost and Found, and Then Lost

My clutch bag I got in France is seen by others as a feminine accessory. I purchased this pouch during my last few hours in Paris after I stuffed my luggage so full you would not open the suitcase without the risk of it exploding. I parked my car at an Indigo parking lot in the Second arrondissement—all packed and ready to go. I checked out of the hotel I was staying at. I brought all my bags to the car. I was getting prepared to drive the rental car back through the busy streets.

I was ready to leave, but before I did this alarm inside of me began to go off. I did little to no shopping for myself during my 1-month stay. I realized whatever I bought, I would inevitably have to wear. It was one of those ridiculously humid days in late August. I walked into the first vintage store and began to look around.

I was looking around the first store for close to an hour. I wanted to walk away with the best item in the store. The salesperson pointed me to the vintage denim rack and I tried on some items per their suggestion. I wanted to only get one outerwear piece to wear to the airport—so be it if I am drenched in sweat before I board. I found a Hugo Boss windbreaker, color-blocked with turquoise-blue and lemon-yellow hues—perfectly faded, an XL neon time capsule from the 1980s. I decided to pick the worn-in neon jacket over the less eccentric denim. Happy with my purchase, I slipped on the jacket—already beginning to feel the heat, under the impression this would be my last purchase in France.

As I was walking back to Indigo, there was another vintage store across the street calling my name. I really should have begun driving already to ensure airport check-in goes smoothly. I couldn't help myself. I quickly took stock of the space I had in my carry-on and ran to the second store to find something slender enough to squeeze into my backpack.

Wearing the jacket I just bought, I looked around at the second store. I quickly found the leather bag basket, where everything was ten euros. I found what I was looking for, the leather clutch from my dreams. It was a perfect rectangle, dark brown, made from the best-smelling alligator leather with a little metal clasp that clicked it shut, something I was considering gifting to my sister, my mom, or my friend Sasha. I actually kept this purchase for myself, cherishing it for only a few weeks. Unfortunately, someone stole the clutch after I dropped it at the bagel shop. I lost it earlier this week, and since then, I have missed it tremendously, unable to accept it's really gone.

I started wearing purses back in 2020. It was freeing to no longer be surrounded by Connecticut-toxic-masculinity where it was common to be judged as a man for wearing such a feminine item and uncommon for a man to even have one in addition to my fear of being judged romantically by people who are not interested in a purse-bearing fem-boy. Since I left this environment three years ago, I said to myself 'Why not?'

I think others view handbags more as a feminine accessory than I do, strangers, family members, and friends included. In New York, I would frequently wear my XL black hoodie when I was riding my skateboard. It caused onlookers to do a double-take when I had my purse with me. To present yourself as a masculine guy (baggy clothes and skateboard) and see it mixed with what a lot of people associate solely for women; a purse, would create a reaction within some people causing them to not know what to do with their feelings and land on spewing hate speech towards me. It happened more times than I would care to remember—more often with my purse.

I think I admire bags simply for their practicality as well as my freedom to wear them—finally being in New York City. I don't consider bags to be gendered, even though a part of me knows just how gendered they are. I once got upset at my friend for calling my bag "a man-purse". I told her "If I was wearing a dress, you wouldn't call it a man-dress." To me it's just a bag, occasionally a purse, and a lot of the time can be my number one form of expression.

Maximiliano De Paz—Perfume

In more recent years, I've learned the importance of self-directed investments. Whether that be a getting a gym membership, or starting a skin care routine, or even taking a daily shower. Although it may appear like these acts are neutrally gendered, I believe that many of these actions can be considered leaning feministic. From personal connotation as a Latino kid, my definition of self-care was showering every once in a while and using hair gel to slick back your hair in the morning. It wasn't until I was older that my definition of self-care was mostly influenced by my father and brother who have more conservative approaches in life.

One object that I use on an almost daily basis is perfume. Perfume is an important part of my day and is often used as my confidence boost for the day. One of my favorite scents in my assortment of fragrances is French Waltz by Golf Le Fleur. Although this scent is a unisex scent made to be worn by all genders, many of my peers have told me that is smells like an old lady. On one hand, my mom loved the scent at first sniff. From that day forward, she would sneak in my room and spray some of it on herself before leaving for work. On the other hand, my brother was immediately indifferent to the fragrance just because of the bottle. The perfume's main notes are floral which are evidenced by the gigantic teal cap in the shape of a flower pedal. He was immediately disgusted when test spraying it and has never picked it back up again since then.

I think this is a great example of how scents and shapes can be immediately associated with one gender over the other. Although scents are subjective, my brother is a 90s baby and grew up in an environment where none of the male figures in his life were open to the idea of a man wearing a floral scent. His personal connotations with what he grew up with don't align with using a perfume with a floral cap and that's perfectly normal. Since a young age, we are accustomed to learning that girls like flowers and that only girl receive flowers. If I were to encounter this perfume bottle at a younger age, I probably also would've figured that it would be on my mom's drawer and not my dad's.

The reality is anyone can wear a perfume like French Waltz. Although many socially established norms prohibit masculine men from wearing a perfume like this, the truth is that shapes and scents are all subjective. I can be a straight man and wear perfume and that's perfectly fine. Neither gender nor sexuality should discredit humans from putting on what they feel best in, whether that be clothes, or perfumes, or makeup. Although I am also guilty of being hypocritical to many objects being gendered, I continue to learn the importance of objects in our daily lives and how gender barriers are all nonexistent.

Maya Urbina—My Motorcycle

Motorcycles, like many other items, have been subject to gendered associations. Historically, motorcycles have often been symbols of masculinity, embodying feelings of freedom, rebellion, and adventure. This image is encouraged through media, advertising, and popular culture, featuring predominantly male riders in a rugged and rebellious context, while women will be on the bike of their bikes and often sexualized. Men are the typical owners and riders of motorcycles.

I always grew up around motorcycles, my dad getting me on one as soon as I could start driving. I finally bought my first motorcycle this past October, and I was through the roof. I was ready to take on the world, feeling as confident as ever being a woman on a motorcycle, especially with my dad encouraging me to be a strong, independent woman. Something I was not prepared for was having my spirit crushed because I slowly realized how male-dominant the motorcycle community was and how some of them aren't as welcoming to women.

Now, entering more specifically into the subcultures of bikes, sometimes women aren't as welcome or they're very rare. I met a new friend at an all female garage this winter, Gail. She is one of the only other women I know that rides, and she also rides a Harley Davidson Chopper like me. Choppers are a niche style of motorcycle that women typically don't ride because they are a more masculine style. Her and I have both been customizing our bikes to be in that style and taking them out when we can.

We bonded recently over being extremely happy that we have each other in such a male-heavy community. Because even though we are riding the same bikes as the men are, we always get told we are doing something wrong. Gail often gets told that her bike looks great, but men will always nitpick something about the style, or the pipes, or the wheels. Her and I can also be the butt of a joke between the men as well, just because they assume we don't know anything about our bikes. Men can also take this opportunity of seeing a woman on a bike, and use that chance to flirt or harass us in different ways. Men will also often assume our sexualities. While I identify as bisexual, and Gail as straight, men will see us together and assume we are together sexually or in a relationship because we are two women on masculine bikes. This leads to crude and inappropriate comments as well.

Quite honestly, yes I see objects and see them as gendered, but often I won't let that guide my decision on if I do or don't want to interact with it. Yes, motorcycles are male-gendered, and they probably always will be with the dominance of men in the community and its history. One thing I will do is try to break those stereotypes. I'm not trying to necessarily make the motorcycle a female-gendered item or make one style more feminine, it's more about wanting to have the motorcycle be something anyone can ride to feel that freedom, independence, and excitement. I don't take riding as just a hobby anymore; it's an action of breaking gender boundaries to open up that confidence, and free-spiritedness to anyone, not just men, or women. Motorcycles are for everyone.

Assignment #5 (Informal "Low Stakes")—Institutional Objects

Amy Diop—The Shop

Here you are looking at a Butthole Surfers album promotion poster from 1996. Butthole Surfers is an experimental rock band from Texas that experienced its peak in the 80s and 90s. This is an original print and not a remake; its rarity and importance are signified by the frame it sits in and its lack of access for sale. This poster lives in a small vintage store in the Lower East Side. The store has been open for a little over ten years now, but everything that is in the shop comes from their archive studio space. In the archives lives the owner's collection of vintage music/movie posters, cultural knick-knacks, and mostly designer and non-designer clothing. Everything in the owner's collection is representative of niche cultural groups he has lived through or secondhand idly experienced growing up in the New York City/Northeast Tri-state area.

The Owner started to collect in his late teen years and is still now in his early forties. He has spent the last twenty years of his life collecting and selling goods to clients from all sorts of backgrounds. Before opening his shop in 2012, the owner strictly did business out of his archive. Brands like Supreme, Stussy and other New York local streetwear brands are a few of many of his clients who would shop his archive for reference for their new collections. His curation is incredibly strong and one is hard to mimic. This Butthole Surfers poster is one of the many posters in the store that customers constantly ask if they can purchase, but he will never get rid of it because it holds so much value to him, and he fears he will never find another. The shop does an interesting thing many for-profit stores do not do. They protect what they honor no matter what price you name if they want to keep it they will keep it. This is what makes them cross into an institution to me because their main focus is preservation first.

Essay #2 (Formal "High Stakes")—Institutional Collections

Eliza Wicks—Hundred Acre Woods

Our first toys were woodchips. Abundantly accessible on the playground, they could become whatever we wanted to be; a cell phone, (a popular choice), a dagger, a drawing tool, food. The sky, or rather the ground, was the limit. Outside, everything was a toy. We spent countless afternoons sharpening sticks into swords, creating friends out of rocks with scrawled on faces, collecting husks, sticking maple seeds to our noses. These were our original toys. Yet, I knew there was a difference between these crafted objects, imbued with imagination to make up for their distinctive lack of functionality, and *real toys*. Inside, there were real toys; games, dolls, cars, and figures designed specifically for our entertainment. Manufactured, shiny, plastic, they felt so separate from the objects we found that brought just as much joy to our lives.

My favorite books and stories always took place in a time before mine, the days of homemade everything; DIY houses, self-churned butter, farmed or hunted food, and toys of the same fashion, corn husk dolls, whittled figures, and marbles. Toys stuck in a separate category between imaginary and manufactured, they fascinated me and created a distance between us and these historical children in my head.

It wasn't until I viewed the original Winnie the Pooh collection, displayed at the Schwarzman branch of the New York Public Library since 1987, that this distinction between past and present began to change. Faded and greying due to time, but clearly well-loved, the original friends of Hundred Acre Woods were like something dug up from plushie catacombs. What had so long in my mind been bright colorful images, distorted over time into sanitized, airbrushed characters and soft, cuddly recreations, were before me in their natural form: coarse, rough, canvas lined and matted fur Frankensteined together with obvious stitches, patchy paw pads, and manes of yarn. They were imperfect. Once a luxurious gift, sold by an esteemed London department store, they now seemed like mere scraps.

Looking at this motley crew of lovable characters, I could see the convergence of the past and present. The limitations of the time apparent in their materials and construction, but also the recognizable characters that had shaped my own childhood. And through these toys, I could imagine myself in the shoes of Christopher Robin, conducting meetings in my room with a round table of plushies or choreographing arguments that existed solely in my head about which animal received more attention. The nature of childhood remains the same despite changes in the world around us, our ties to material objects that we infuse with life creating a new reality for us to live in.

Winnie the Pooh was a staple of my childhood and it is strange to imagine that before he was mine, before he became the friendly sweet toothed yellow bear that is printed on clothes, recreated in plushie form, and even tattooed on people's bodies, he was just another boy's best friend.

Growing up I never had a favorite plushie or toy to fill the shoes of the title "best friend." Used to looking after myself from a young age, I was comfortable in the worlds of my imagination, alone but not lonely. I lived out my fantasies of companionship and a different life through the books I read or movies I watched. I went for walks in the woods and carried out top secret missions with my team of spies, crossed into magical lands, ran a boarding school out of my room, anything I could imagine was possible. I thought of myself like Christopher Robin, content with the creations of my own concoction. Little did I know we weren't living the same experience as I had so naively hoped.

Christopher the character and Christopher the boy lived vastly different lives. I felt myself close to the idealized, fictional little boy, surrounded by silly but lovable friends rather than the child sent off to school, bullied for his father's success. Knowing this, his worn-down bear carries a heavier aura, looking out from behind its glass display cage. He has watched the thousands of tourists who flock to the library and marvel over the familiar character, taking pictures before walking away without a thought of the little boy to whom he was once tied. Once again, the spotlight has found its way back to the bear and this time, he is the one with a story to tell.

He longs to shout that the misadventures of Winnie the Pooh and his friends are not just the innocent fantasies of a young boy. They are invention of a distant father who created an idealized relationship with his son through the only thing he knew: writing. He has a story to tell that has been pushed aside for a brighter narrative, dormant for the past 100 years as his name has accumulated a worth in the billions. Imagination is a powerful thing and can bring even the most worthless, ordinary objects, like woodchips, to life. It can create stories and worlds to embellish our current reality or construct a new one entirely. Before I had anything, I had my imagination and that was enough. But for others, like Christopher Robin, one man's imagination was the very thing that soured his relationship with the one friend that was solely his.

Looking back on my own childhood, I am grateful for the innocence with which I played freely in my own world. Pooh bears tired, slumping, shape, reminds me not to take granted the magic I experienced without the company of friends, real or manufactured. His days of providing comfort are over, his little boy long gone, his name and image since altered to cater to the masses. He has lost his original purpose and now sits on a podium with his original crew, a new purpose instilled in his worn limbs.

He is a reminder of our earliest days, the days where objects were just as dear to us as the people in our lives, of imaginary friends and days spent carelessly, without the worries that come with growing up. He is also a reminder of his first friend, the reason for his legacy and fame and now his seat in the box. A reminder that before there was a bear, there was a boy.

Scott Krupa—Charles Dickens' Desk + Creativity

My first thought when we whizzed past Charles Dickens' desk, was why the person who was touring our group did not call attention to the desk. The objects on display at the Polansky Treasures Exhibit at the New York Public Library, ranged in some of the most fascinating objects that I have ever come across. All the objects being presented in the same room together, making our tour combined with the background information that much better. From the hand painted Studio 54 invitation for Trumann Capote, made by overly enthusiastic Andy Warhol, a few paces away religious artifacts and other historical documents—like a handwritten version of the *Bill of Rights*. There were more objects in the space that required further explanation and historical context,than the time we had available to look.

Charles Dickens' desk is one of those personal items that potentially is the one closest object to Dickens and his writings. For example, at the end of the Patti Smith book, *Just Kids*, she shows a picture of a young girl working at Robert Mapplethorpe's old desk from when they were together. After publishing *Just Kids* in January 2010, Patti was contacted by the person who bought Robert's desk at auction. For her, it was an extremely moving and powerful image, of the buyer's daughter working at Robert's desk—the same desk that Patti worked at in their early years together. Seeing this picture at the end of her memoir was heart wrenching. The previous section at the end of the book is where Patti explains to the audience Robert's AIDS diagnosis and Robert's jokes with Patti about the length of her hair and how it showed time had passed.

In the midst of his worsening condition at the end of his life, the desk meant the world to Patti due to the fact it contained so many memories of Robert Mapplethorpe's and Patti's, shared, early life together. They promised each other when they were young and full of dreams that they would stay together no matter what, with the verbalized goal of helping the other find success—never leaving the other behind. The most incredible part of this story was they were able to fulfill their promises to each other.

Eventually, the romantic aspect of the relationship would die. They were still living together at the Hotel Chelsea, pretending to be in a relationship with the public in reality one living on one side of the loft, and the other the opposite. The both of them were aware that they both started seeing other people—something kept hidden from the public for some time. Shortly after, Robert struggled with accepting his homosexuality at the end of their romantic relationship, after being confronted by Patti.

The desk is how the book ends, showing directly the relationship between the object, Robert Mapplethorpe, and his creativity. Tragically, Robert Mapplethorpe passed away from HIV, AIDS at the young age of 42. I see his desk as an extension of his life, and to see it in use and appreciated is clearly something I feel would make someone like Robert smile if he was still here with us. Even though Robert was a photographer and not a writer, his object has context to someone like Patti, who is able to fully express the emotional relevance from the object into words.

For someone like Dickens who built his career for himself as a writer, the object of a desk is that much more relevant to him and his writing career, making it a better fit for a NYPL historical archive. It was interesting to see all the different details on Dickens' desk. For example, the raised border that goes around the back of the desk like a small fence. His lamp and the analog calendar stuck out to me the most. My reaction to the aesthetic of his desk was it is surprisingly intricate while maintaining its simplicity, including the raised portion that is angled towards the desk chair. Everything had practical use and was not distracting. I would love to have seen what it looked like while it was in use.

Was Dickens a cluttered worker? Or was he extremely neat? When I work best I tend to clean everything in the eyeview. After I do that, I can feel free to make a mess while I work—allowing me as much freedom as I would like, geginning with a blank slate each time I clean. Dickens wrote classics at that desk and hopefully the desk was the ideal object to set him off into a state of flow. I believe that he was successfully able to do so if was able to make so many classics at that very desk.

When I was working out of a 2 bedroom apartment in New York for a couple months. I made the second room my designated art studio equipped with my roommate's old desk and a half sofa. The room almost instantaneously became the designated flow spot. This was a time in New York when I first got here, and was not in school. My sleep schedule was flipped upside down, and I found myself staying up until 5 and 6 am. I was starting to develop my painting abilities and was creating art that would become the foundation to the paintings I am selling now. I would first get into the studio around 11 or 12 in the middle of the night if I couldn't sleep or was antsy. Time would stand still when I was working, and finding a medium that allowed me to get "in the zone" was likely a large part of why I fell in love with painting professionally.

I distinctly remember the night where I made the first pair of chef pants. These hand- painted pants, with an abstraction of a chef textile, were based on my work in restaurants. When I picked up the paintbrush for the first time, the thought of the hours and minutes required to achieve the look I had in mind, at the time seemed daunting and tediously repetitive. I would play music and watch *Arrested Development* at the same time, allowing the process to become less intimidating. That first pair I made was in anticipation the night before a concert in Brooklyn. I was up until the morning and didn't see the sun rise. Placing the finishing touches on the pants,I was absolutely floored that I unintentionally worked for at least 6 hours straight after being awake all day. The next day was the concert and I was really excited to wear my pants for the first time out and about; they were even reeking of paint odor in the best way. When I was there I had no idea if my date or anyone would even notice that I painted them. To my surprise I was bombarded with compliments and comments from strangers the whole night—the whole time there felt surreal. From their feedback I could see lightning in a bottle. I thought to myself that night if I was wearing pants that said GUCCI legibly and in all caps all up and down the legs in New York, or better yet at Baby's All Right in Brooklyn (where the concert was held) no one would say a word. Just because they can read and interpret what you are wearing doesn't mean they are going to go out of their way to compliment you. After that experience I continued making different iterations and eventually would scale up to larger canvas paintings. If I wasn't immersed in a flow state in the studio in the middle of the night, I wouldn't be working on the same projects and events I am able to work on now.

This is what led me to having the book *Flow* become one of my most internalized and appreciated explanations of how my creativity operates—gaining a scientific understanding of why I can't put the brushes down in the process. Mihaly Robert Csikszentmihalyi was a Hungarian-American psychologist who wrote the book *Flow*. He is recognized for and named the psychological concept of "flow". Flow is defined as the melting together of action and consciousness; the state of finding a balance between a skill and how challenging that task is.

I finished this book after experiencing constant long periods of flow, in that studio, for the first time in my life. For someone with my level of ADHD, it was virtually unheard of for me to focus on something for 2, 4, up to 8 hours. I am talking about locked in focus the whole time too. This is what would happen when I would be creating in this studio and felt freed to be working constantly because it did not feel like work. It did not feel like productivity either, rather, it felt I was doing something unproductive in a sense. If you have a massive body of work, most likely you are creative and you don't necessarily have your priorities adjusted to being extraordinarily productive. If there is this energy and voice to write an entire book or complete 100 painting, until you sit down in a space where that's even possible to do so, it is difficult to let your imagination run free. That is the secret to flow; It never necessarily feels like work when you're doing it (even if it is). You can use flow in even the most mundane of activities, making it more exciting and to get in the zone.

For a dancer the object could be the Adidas track pants that allow the dancer to feel free in their movements. In the book *Flow*, the author expands on the idea of using dancers as an example of flow. There is a passage that describes how a decision that happens in the matter of seconds can feel much longer, describing the reverse of "time flying", where it can actually slow down for certain actions. Csikszentmihalyi wrote "Ballet dancers describe how a difficult turn that takes less than a second in real timestretches out for what seems like minutes". This goes to show the different experiences of flow with all types of professions, hobbies and tasks.

I see Dickens' desk similarly to how an artist in the studio experiences many hours passing as if they were only working for a couple of minutes. It is a tool that may or may not assist in inducing a flow state, one rooted in materiality, and the closest distance from his genius and creative thought.

Krystal Magliulo—The Radical Queen

Before we officially moved in together this winter, my girlfriend and I spent our summers doing long distance. We dreaded it. It wasn't even the worst situation in the world. I mean, we didn't even live more than three hours apart, but there's a reason the term "U-Haul lesbian" is less of a joke and more of a serious term in our community. It's extremely real. The 81 miles between Centereach, New York and Farmington, Connecticut felt like countries apart, and every time Sophie and I left each other, we sobbed as though we would never see each other again. All these waterworks, and yet, we knew we probably only had 72 hours in us until we would hop on a ferry and cross the Long Island Sound to be together again. I thought of it as romantic, but our family and friends would probably consider it dramatic.

To soften the pain of being torn apart by our terrible, minimum-wage, seasonal cashier jobs, we decided to use the summer to create our little lesbian book club, just the two of us. Whenever we weren't together, we would fly through novels about forbidden lesbian romance and the history of our community. Sometimes, finding these lesbian books was even more strenuous than spending time apart: Out of print, unpopular—you name it, it seemed like no one wanted to carry lesbian books these days.

Our saving grace was Steve, Sophie's dad, who most definitely has an unlabeled hoarding problem. In their family basement lives rows and rows of oak wooden bookshelves that touch the ceiling, all caving in at the middle, ready to give out from the weight of the hardcovers they are sheltering. Unemployed and obsessed with his collections, Steve took the task of finding us a quality queer novel to kick off our very serious summer reading. He claimed he knew just the book, and reflecting back, he did. It didn't take him long to pull out a first edition copy of (my now, all-time favorite) novel, *Stone Butch Blues* by Leslie Feinberg. He may be a hoarder, but even through all the piles of chaos, he can locate any one of his beloved items. Steve graciously lent us his copy of the book, but made us swear we wouldn't fold the page edges or spill anything on the cover. Apparently, barely any stores sold the book anymore and as a collector myself, I completely understood the anxiety of parting with one of your precious items for a few weeks. We promised to look after it and keep it safe.

Reading *Stone Butch Blues* was a whirlwind of emotions. It was all that occupied my brain for weeks. The print was fine and the pages were lengthy, but I chugged on like someone was going to steal the book right out of my hands if I didn't finish it soon. So much history that I was unaware of flooded the pages, and I felt addicted to uncovering more and more. When I finished reading, Feinberg's storytelling lingered in my mind all summer. My girlfriend and I referenced it nonstop and overanalyzed the pages until they could no longer be interpreted any further. Steve never received his copy back. It proudly lives on our pink, thrifted bookshelf that sits in the corner of our bedroom. I'm sorry Steve. Maybe when you turn into a lesbian, you can have it back.

Ever since *Stone Butch Blues*, I have been chasing the feeling of discovering lesbian and queer media that is as enriching and fulfilling, but I haven't found anything that compares. I've stalked the visitation page of the Lesbian Herstory Archives website for months, but have had no luck securing an appointment. I had come to the sad conclusion that I wouldn't be visiting anytime soon. Sophomore year of college, I wrote a massive paper about this in my Women's Writing class, but the erasure of lesbian history and stories proved to be both very real and very inaccessible. Clearly, this issue is ongoing, and considering today's political climate, I can't say I have much hope for improvement anytime soon.

On one of the first summery and warm Tuesdays of March in New York City, I walked towards Bryant Park to meet up with my classmates, where we would experience the New York Public Library's Treasures Collection. I wasn't expecting to stumble upon any objects that spoke to this topic I care so deeply about. Truthfully, it didn't even cross my mind. I guided myself through the exhibit freely, gravitating towards art projects created by women and raggedy, but charming, stuffed animals that inspired Winnie the Pooh. It wasn't until I reached the newer "Banned: Censorship and the Freedom to Read" display that drew me in entirely.

I locked eyes with the smallest item on display. A zine—probably 6 x 9, brought to life on powdery, baby blue-colored construction paper. My gaze followed the swooping, imperfect bubble letters that graced the front page, spelling out, *The Radical Queen*. Intertwined with the Sharpied letters was a sketch of a feminine being, with long, thick hair and fluttering eyelashes. Outlining her silhouette, followed by capital letters, was a saying: "DEDICATED TO THE QUEENS WHO

STARTED IT ALL." This struck me. So many of my role models and comfort artists are drag queens, like Sasha Colby and Gottmik, who use their platform for good, blurring gender lines and defying societal expectations to showcase the power of embracing one's identity. Above the sketch were more words, this time typed in a type-writer style font: "THE MAGAZINE OF THE NON-MAN." As described in the blurb beneath the zine, "Many gay liberation movements of the 1970s, such as Gay Activists Alliance, were not necessarily welcoming of femmes, drag queens, transgender, or other gender nonconforming people. At the same time, several factions of the feminist movement were also opposed to drag and transgender identities." It seemed to me that *The Radical Queen* was built for everyone, and I liked that. Desperate to flip through its pages, I bombarded the Special Collections Specialists with questions on how I could access the item. Their directions seemed simple enough. Create a library card in-person, make an online appointment, request the specific item, and show up to the library when you're told. As I rode the A train home to Brooklyn from Penn Station, I followed the library's simple instructions and located their digital calendar of available appointments. Perfect, the morning before my Tuesday afternoon class.

Two days later, I received a follow up email from a research guide named Malika who informed me that the digital calendar was not accurate, and that my Tuesday time slot was actually non-existent. They wrote to me in a short and sweet reply, "We are sorry for the inconvenience. You may try again and select an appointment for another day," Unfazed by this mishap, I walked myself through the library's appointment-making process once again and scrolled through their availability, which was very limited to say the least. Either the appointments were simply taken or just extremely impossible for a college student with five classes and a part time job to squeeze into their schedule. The research room I would be visiting, The Brooke Russell Astor Reading Room for Rare Books and Manuscripts, was only open from Tuesday to Saturday, between 11am and 5pm. I played with the idea of ditching a class so I could finally come face to face with this zine, but decided against it. If I ran fast enough, I should be able to have a brief, hour-long visit in between my morning and afternoon Thursday classes. I submitted the application to verify my appointment and hoped for the best.

Another two days had passed, and yet again, I received another rejection. Malika explained what I already knew, that the calendar was inaccurately updated and that Thursday actually had no accessible appointments. Begging for a better solution, especially considering I was running out of time to further explore this object for the sake of this paper, I asked Malika if they could personally create an appointment for me. An appointment they would be actually sure existed would be preferable. They agreed that doing it that way would be for the best and based on my schedule, I was set to finally read *The Radical Queen* on a Friday morning, only two hours before I would clock into my waitressing shift at Chelsea Market, serving warm pita bread sandwiches to eager tourists with growling stomachs. Two hours may seem like a lot of time to some, especially my late-to-everything girlfriend, but the thought of having only 120 minutes to check in at the library, analyze the zine carefully and thoughtfully, and rely on the almost always delayed subway to get me to work on time, made my skin crawl in anxiety hives. But I can handle one hectic morning, I told myself.

More groggy than normal, I arrived at the New York Public Library bright and early, one hour before my appointment time to ensure that I could smoothly check in my coat and print my physical library card before being set up to view this zine. That all went according to plan and like a nerd, I hovered near the front door of the Reading Room at 10:50 like a teenage girl queuing to see her favorite artist in concert. I picked away at my cuticles anxiously, triple checking on my phone that the subway from Bryant Park to Chelsea market was still running on time. Everything was still going to plan.

At 11 on the dot, I was let into the enchanting study hall. For a moment, I stood in the coziness of the warm, golden brown lighting and the hundreds of tightly packed books housed in glass cases, acting as wallpaper that added character to the room. Breaking me out of my trance, a worker sitting at a check-in desk questioned, "First time?" I shyly nodded as I met them in the middle of the room. Waiting for my arrival was a stack of unsigned paperwork with a New York Public library-themed pen. After verbally going over the rules, I sloppily scribbled my signature on the blank line to promise that I would never misuse, mistreat, or steal these precious objects. After signing, I was directed to meet another employee at a much longer desk, that was placed against the back wall and surrounded by gray boxes of all different sizes.

At this desk, I was to check in again, reminding them of my name, my appointment time, which object I had a date with. After confirming all these details, the librarian began to rummage through the boxes of resources, attempting to locate mine: Box 415 of the NYPL'S Lesbian, Gay, Bisexual, and Transgender Periodical Collection. There were a fair amount of boxes waiting to be united with their researcher, probably around 35, but after watching the librarian triple check each box for "415," I found myself recalculating how much time I would have to examine my object. Turning their attention back towards me, I noticed the puzzled look that had crept onto their face. "This is so strange, I can't seem to find your box," they finally expressed. Pressed for time, I imagine my girlfriend beside me, laughing and teasing me for thinking I still wouldn't have enough time. The thought of my girlfriend's lack of seriousness helped calm me for a moment as the librarian searched for a coworker to solve this mystery with. They told me to take a seat.

I felt quite professional as I seated myself at a wooden desk with a large, overhead light attached to it. I was surrounded by other researchers, who were probably much smarter than me, doing something actually cool with their lives, like writing a novel or curing some disease, rather than struggling to make it to their waitressing shift on time. Just like we would if we were in a classroom, we all sat with our desks in a row. Swinging my legs back and forth underneath the desk out of boredom, I found myself trying to make eye contact with the librarians. After one of them glanced over at me, they quickly fluttered their eyes towards the ground. God, this can't be good. They're trying to avoid me.

I kept looking in their direction, hoping they would cave to the awkwardness of being stared at, or that I could maybe pick up on their hushed whispers about where my zine was. After all, it was pretty much completely silent in the Reading Room. Finally, at 11:40 a worker approached me awkwardly and spoke softly, "We are trying to locate your box, but it seems like someone has mislocated it. It may be completely somewhere else in the building, but we will keep you updated. Sorry." Not trying to come off as rude, I held my exasperated sigh until the librarian was back to typing away on their computer. This can't be happening to me right now.

For another 30 minutes, I sat stressed, bouncing my legs from nervousness, fearing that I wouldn't come to know my item at all. This experience only fulfilled my prophecy further: It is absolutely impossible to get your hands on lesbian media, even at the library that has promised to keep it in safekeeping. In the middle of this thought, I was interrupted by a sudden plop in front of me. Thank the Lesbian Gods. It was Box 415.

I double tapped my phone. 10 minutes. At this point, I didn't care about how many minutes I had with *The Radical Queen*, I just wanted a glimpse of its contents.

Reminding myself that, even though I was in a major rush, I couldn't carelessly flip through the pages, I composed myself and carefully lifted the cover with my pinkie finger. Page one. An accurate *Alice and Wonderland* doodle with the words, "gender is the caste system by which male-DOMINATED $OCIETY designates Women & effeminates as inferior!" sitting on top of Alice's bow. I was intrigued by the messy mix of inconsistent capitalization and the dollar sign that replaced the "s" in society. Definitely intentional. Page two. A lengthy, authorless piece titled "on being a woman", which went on for ten pages. Considering the day's unfortunate chain of events, I knew I didn't have time to sit and read through it all, even though I actually wanted to. I scanned the typewriter font and landed my eyes a few paragraphs in. This mystery writer and I connected through their words, "I hated my adolescent years. All my friends kept talking about males as though they were the only reason to exist. (For me, they were a reason to stop existing)." I couldn't put a face to this person, or even a name, but I certainly related to them—especially my high school self. I wish I had something like this to read when I was trying to battle my lesbianism at seventeen. I probably would've stopped trying to suppress how I was feeling. Funny enough, this zine most definitely existed when I was seventeen. It was published in 1973, a year before my parents were even born. But of course, if the raging lesbian version of myself can't even find specific lesbian books I want to read from the library, Barnes & Noble, or on eBay, there's no way the closeted version of me could've dug up and located a copy of *The Radical Queen*, as helpful and cool as that would've been. The New York Public Library staff and I could barely handle completing that mission today.

Other personal stories filled these pages, some credited to their authors, while others seemed to want to remain anonymous. Makes sense. Under pressure, I struggled to snap pictures of the pages I couldn't pause to glimpse at because of the time. I'd read them later at home, in my bed, zooming in on the grainy photos. Better than nothing. Passing over doodled, queer-coded comic strips and quotes from Virgina Woolf, I make it to the final few pages of this edition of *The Radical Queen*.

"THE RADICAL QUEEN is free but we need donations desperately. We survive only through your generosity. We are poor." This statement is so blunt and I love it because it rings true, even today. There is no sugar coating that the LGBTQ+ struggles when it comes to fighting for our funding, visibility, and support. Even in 2025, I couldn't gain access to visit any of the objects that live in The Lesbian Herstory Archives. Their archive is maintained solely by volunteers and the organization can't afford to hire a huge team of people to carefully preserve and curate our history. Honestly, lack of funding is probably partially part of the reason why Box 415 went missing at the New York Public Library for almost two hours. I'm sure many of the librarians take on more responsibilities than their job descriptions require, all to provide the public with their right to education. All my frustrations from the day melt away. At least, I am lucky enough to hold some LGBTQ+ history in my hands. Even if it was just for a few minutes.

On the last page of the zine, is a bolded section titled, "Information of Interest:" It is filled entirely with contact information and phone numbers of organizations that our community can reach out to for support, like the Lesbian Hotline (Women Only) and Gay Activists Alliance. A small blurb explains that the Gay Students Temple & Gay Women Temple have a coffee hour on Wednesdays for those who want to connect together, in person. There's a phone number for more details.

When I get home, I dial SA9-2001, the number I memorized for the Lesbian Hotline. I didn't know such a thing existed or what the hotline could exactly offer. Maybe advice? Maybe event information to meet other lesbians? I wanted to find out, but my hopes were crushed. The phone number was no longer in service. That would've been so cool. I wonder if something similar still exists for lesbians today. I make note to research it later.

Flipping through *The Radical Queen* made me feel so comforted as I gained a deeper understanding of how our community best connected decades ago. While today we have reality shows like *RuPaul's Drag Race* streaming on MTV and artists like Chappell Roan singing about lesbian situationships on pop radio, as much exposure as possible will always be necessary. We need to ensure that everyone in this country who feels unsupported or misunderstood has access to a place where they can find their people, and to be themselves. I feel grateful that the New York Public Library gave me a taste of one of these spaces our community had in the 70s. While it might've been a messy process getting my hands on *The Radical Queen*, it's just a reminder to keep putting in the work to tell our stories and preserve our history, because no one else is going to do it for us.

Assignment #8 (Informal "Low Stakes")—Trash

Emily Bunch—Trash?

When you google the definition of trash, as many might do to discover their limitations when being assigned this assignment, there is actually two definitions that come up. The first one talks basically about things that have been discarded. The second one mentions a person.

This could be why when I told my best friend about this assignment she instead sent me pictures of people we know and told me I should write about them. I am sorry to disappoint anyone looking for an intense gossiping session, but I chose not to write about them, although I absolutely would have loved to. Maybe this is called being mature, I am not sure.

But the truth of the matter is that discarded should be used very loosely in the definition of trash. What does it mean to discard trash? You and I are probably picturing neatly tying it up in a bag, putting it in a can, etc. Unfortunately, discarding just means getting rid of it. And as we know in NYC, this often means on the street.

Maybe New York City is just dirty because we use it. Or maybe there are a lot more systematic problems at work here, one of the smaller ones being the immense lack of trash cans in the entire city. You could walk 10 blocks and not see one trash can, or if you're lucky, see one that is overflowing. Maybe as humans in a city with extremely limited space, we simply do not have the resources and space to support the amount of trash we create. I am not expert at any of this, but I think I agree with all of this. I also do not feel qualified to discuss the other issues that may contribute to the littering problem in this city so let's just pretend that my trash can idea is absolutely groundbreaking.

Most of the time, the streets of the city are just gross. They smell. You probably occasionally step on garbage, or unfortunately worse, do it every day. My specific photograph is mild, much worse exists.

So when I stumbled on smashed bottles, I was not at all surprised. Curiosity has been bugging me; maybe this bottle was smashed after the Knicks won Sunday afternoon, (as this pic was taken near Madison Square Garden). Maybe this person just could not handle their excitement over the idea that the Knicks might actually make it to the second round of the playoffs (for the first time since 2013). Okay, enough sports talk; I highly doubt that is what actually happened.

Maybe, this bottle was smashed on accident, ran over by a car or bike. I hope it didn't pop their tire because that would suck. Maybe someone threw it on purpose. Were they mad? Maybe they were in an intensely angry phone conversation. They could have been talking to their ex-wife, their brother, their lawyer . . . the possibilities are endless. Were they trying to hurt someone? Maybe someone was protecting themselves. I wonder if someone accidentally stepped on it after the fact. What if the glass went through their shoe and cut them? Maybe the glass was just dropped by someone who was sick of walking with it, with no sign of a trash can. Or maybe this is just remnants of trash left on the street after garbage collection (much more likely).

Regardless, there is definitely a story of who was drinking the several beverages smashed across the sidewalk. Even more unfortunate, this is not a rare sight in New York City, so my advice would be to watch where you are walking. I hope you don't step on glass, that doesn't sound fun.

Amy Diop—Trash

I love trash. I always have and always will. I grew up low-income in New York City in a poorly maintained one bedroom apartment, with half broken unique furniture, living in hand-me-downs. I never really felt that shameful about it though because even though it was all half broken and used I thought everything we had was cool as shit. My mom is incredibly skilled in adding fantasy to everything. She made me see beauty, value, funk, and more in almost everything. Also to her benefit we had and still have similar taste so I truly just loved how many of our things looked no matter how tattered they seemed to others. I love the essence of what trashiness is; thrown to the side, decrepit, dirty, uncared for, negatively said—useless. There is an angst to it that is incredibly interesting and exciting. That's why the concept of trash has always been kind of meaningless to me. It's easy for me to understand our consumerist society, why we consider many more things trash to continue the cycle of retrieving new things to uphold and operate within the system we have built for ourselves through the centuries.

Because of my love for trash I challenged myself not to photograph very obvious types of trash like garbage can, disposable sites, etc. I did this because I knew my writing very quickly would become another man's trash is another man's treasure summary. I constantly preach about the resourcefulness of trash and that almost nothing is trash, especially if you're crafty. I kept thinking about my ashtrays. I look at them multiple times a day, I smoke a lot. My porcelain purple and cream triangle patterned pot-like ash tray is gorgeous to me. It's glossy in a way that almost looks like its glass casted and it hides all the nasty waste from smoking: ash. My other ashtray is still fun to look at and it's stupidly valuable. It was a gift from my boss because he always jokes about my smoking habit. It's a $100 70s Kartell ashtray. I always think about how nasty it has become from all my smoke waste but that's what it's meant to be for. I found the relationship between trash and waste and the things we use to contain it funny. It's almost as if the more lavish the containment is, the grosser and closer to trash the waste is. It made me think about how much waste we create just from our everyday habits like smoking. How do I just unintentionally own a collection of ash because of habits? Then again I am faced with the same question I have been asked all semester, what makes a collection valuable or matter?

Talking about my trash dilemma and spiral I experienced this week, my friend Bowman took me to a scrap yard near his studio to look at some of his favorite trash. The funny thing is we later find out that this trash is most definitely trash unless you pick a favorite of the scrap yard owners. His yard has all the old gating from the outside of Brooklyn homes and he barley spoke to me other than literally saying, "Yah it's all trash unless you want that," and pointed to the one frame I was considering taking, because it's trash right? Thinking about trash is making me feel crazy and confused, because there is no ownership understanding when it comes to trash. Maybe that is what trash is in our society? Trash is when someone does not want to take ownership over a thing that was maybe once theirs or came from them. I realized we experience this lack of common understanding of what trash is all the time. All the awkward moments of "OH NO! DON'T THROW THAT OUT" we experience in our lives show how often trash is poorly defined.

Assignment #9 (Informal "Low Stakes")—Reduce, Reuse, Recycle!

Alexandra Walicke—Vase

When the sun hits it just the right way, the colors of its stained glass project onto the white countertop. It's holy. It has its own aura and pale colors of gold and pink, some more yellow, some more purple. It's the pink that's my favorite.

It was my birthday. My mom sent me flowers. It was during lockdown and I was staying with someone I was dating at the time. I was working until my job closed down, so I didn't want to risk getting her sick. I didn't want to get sick of her either. It kind of just stuck for a while.

I remember thinking the flowers were pretty but I couldn't say what they even looked like anymore. We were on the phone and she asked me if I liked the vase. She told me that she picked it out since she thought i'd like it. I stared at it more than I'd even look at the flowers—it wasn't the florist who chose it, how it was, it was my mom. It's like that she cemented all those pretty pieces of glass onto it herself—just because she chose it, just because she thought of me.

The vase stayed on display, empty. I wanted to keep looking at it. It was too pretty, it felt too special to not. Still during covid, I went back to her house for two months before I moved out for good. I didn't display it when I was with her; I didn't need to—I don't even remember where I kept it.

I didn't have the heart to tell her that I was leaving when I did, so the day I signed the lease was the day I had to rip the bandage off. I waited too long. There were no more days between it and me. Right as I was at the threshold of the door, I leaned back inside and told her. I don't even remember how she reacted, what she said. I just remember how bad I felt, and how free.

She came around when she was helping me pack. She cared more about what I needed there than about it being there. She held up the vase and asked if I wanted to bring it—of course I did. I remember how much it shined as she bubble-wrapped it. The little clear domes refracted its colors, and the room was bright with them. It felt like her love.

When I got there, I knew it was too precious. I couldn't leave it in the kitchen or dining room. I didn't know who was most likely to break it, if it were to happen—the roommates or the cat. I was gambling it that way. So, it needed to be safe. It held paintbrushes and incense, tucked in a corner of my room. It stayed dark.

Four years and three different apartments—that's all it took for it to find its way out of hiding. This third place is different, with different people, different light, air. It didn't need to hide; we were both past that. Still not holding flowers, it found its home with spatulas and spoons. It greets me every morning, every meal.

Here, it shimmers again, usually around noon, when the sun hits it through the skylight.

It's happier now. It's home.

Essay #3 (Formal "High Stakes")– The Things Left Behind

Eliza Wicks–Familiar Strangers

During our summer trips to Korea, going to the public bath was the one tradition that I shared exclusively with my mother and grandmother. A break from translating for my confused American father, from caring for my emotionally volatile brother, or dealing with the progressing stages of my grandfather's Alzheimer's, we all relished these trips. In a large room with other women, we washed off the clinging heat of the summer, sweated out our emotions, and recharged with good old gossip in the large stone baths, ranging from boiling hot to ice cold. The bath brought out a communal vulnerability due to its intimate nature and I loved to imagine my mother at my age, doing the same thing with the women of her family. It was the one tradition that had stood the test of time, despite the working shower in my grandmother's house. Plus, I knew that the moment we went back to the States, we would go back to our solitary American lives and that closeness, that innate connection would be gone. A part of my mother would remain at home in Korea with her family, out of reach until the next year.

The strangest part about growing up with significantly older parents is the realization of how much life they have lived that you will never know about. Sure, I have been given the bare-bones outline of their timelines, a highlight reel to consolidate decades of important moments and days. But the details are missing and I am left with a murky picture that has kept them a distance away, like strangers that I have known for my whole life.

The easiest way for me to gain an understanding into their pasts are through objects and pictures, of which, there seem to never be enough. I am forced to trace backwards into an archaic time before digital preservation and collection. All that is left is what is immediately in my late maternal grandmother's house and mine, the remnants of my father's side scattered to various corners of the United States.

Yet, it feels as the years go on that even these last havens of memory are at risk of extinction. Each year, it feels that more and more are lost and I find myself moving farther away, forgetting details, losing even that initial picture of these people that have raised me.

I feel as though I have been long estranged to my father's past, never experiencing the place where he grew up. My most prominent memories of their family traditions of vacations to Cape May, my grandfather's favorite dessert, or interactions with my cousins are far behind me, back in the days of childhood naivete, characterized by a fierce reliance on my parents. Yet, I am materially closer to their history than I am to my mother's side which sit thousands of miles and an ocean away. My dresser is made from a quarter sawn white oak and previously belonged to my grandmother. Our house used to be filled with furniture like this piece; an end table, a desk, chair, pieces of history that had made it this far. However, over the years they have been replaced with new pieces designed to look rustic and homey, but lacking any of the history or character of their previous counterparts. My dresser is the last remaining piece of this historical puzzle. But to me, it isn't any different from any other secondhand piece of furniture I may have acquired from a thrift store or flea market. I can't picture my grandmother using it, yanking out drawers and slamming them in a rush, accidentally denting or scratching the top, staining water marks into its surface from an errant glass. But despite all this, I cling onto this relic, symbolic of something I don't feel as though I lost because in a sense, I never really had it. Is it really a preservation of my history if I have lost the story or is it just someone else's that I am simply safeguarding?

Although it is my father's archive that seems to be already lost, it is my mother's that I fear of losing. Perhaps this is because I have watched the seemingly rapid deterioration and metamorphosis of what, although far away, was always a constant in my life.

My mother has always been a sort of enigma. No matter how detailed of an account I may receive, the first half of her life will always feel out of reach. She is from a different world than I, and no matter how hard I try I will never be able to fully understand it, just as she will never understand mine. The combined barriers of technology and culture have scrambled the signal to allow me to access her past and the best I can do is parse my way through the limited photos and stories I have.

A few years ago, during an attempt to declutter the years' worth of storage collecting dust in our basement, my parents began a systematic removal of items that had been down there for as long as I can remember. In one of the dressers, long known as the dresser where we keep wrapping paper in the bottom drawers, I found, shoved in the back of an upper drawer, an envelope of old photos. None of the subjects were familiar to me, the pictures all tinged with a rustic washed out look. Until in one photo of a group of people, all sitting around and smiling at the camera, I recognized my mother. She looked different than the woman I have known my whole life. Her hair was longer, blown out without her signature crazy curls, and she wore an 80s windbreaker. I couldn't believe this was my mother, the same woman who teaches speech pathology and goes to church every Sunday and wakes up at 4:30 on most days. Upon flipping through the rest of the photos, I could recognize who I assume to be her first husband. I had only learned of him a few years prior, that he had tragically passed away from an unexpected heart attack. When I had first heard of him, it was shocking and sad, but strangely impersonal. Years ago, in another country, a man of whom I had no knowledge of his face or name, had died. Yet now, seeing these pictures of my young mother, not too much older than me, it hit me. I hadn't wondered why I had never seen photos from this time in my mother's life, the gaps between childhood and adult photos explained away by a cultural or generational difference. For as long as I could remember I was the center of the timeline, the most important years of her life. Anything before hadn't mattered to me or even felt real. But now I wondered if this was the reason a period so significant had been essentially erased from the history books of my mother, because they were a reminder of a loss that was too difficult to preserve.

I think it is this mystery that has for so long and continues to surround my mother which makes the process of material loss so difficult. It feels as though with it I am losing the possibility of ever learning these secrets, these long forgotten or hidden details. Our relationship has long been rocky, this rift making it feel as though I have lost the right to ask, that this side is no longer a part of me. As though our distance is something deeper, due to something within me that is inferior or incomplete. I have always felt internally Korean as that is all I have ever known, the only other place that has felt like home. But my connection to that world, the link that can help me decipher all of the details and mysteries leading back along my family chain has been slowly rusting over and I fear the day it might snap off completely.

Watching my grandparents' house change through their decade long battle with Alzheimer's felt like watching a house slowly sink deeper and deeper into mud before being finally swallowed up, gone without a trace. Items disappeared along with their memories, no longer able to recall the stories behind them, either put into storage or given away. And each summer as I stepped into the house for the first time, there was a difference that I couldn't quite put my finger on. The life became quieter and duller, the house too organized, too clean, too safe, in case of an accident or a fall, of which there were many. I expected their room to feel different after their deaths, emptier, sadder, but it didn't. It looked and felt the same. My family was strangely casual about the whole thing, perhaps because they were prepared because there was nothing left to do. My mother and aunt pulled items out of my grandmother's closet nonchalantly, tossing them on the bed or to me to try on in the mirror. We continued to use her beautiful dishes to eat our breakfasts, her half-used shampoos, her worn in slippers by the stairs. Everything stayed in its proper place as if we would hear the screeching whine of the screen, the sound of the heavy wooden door sliding open, and my grandmother would step right back into her old life. Perhaps if nothing changed, it was a sign that nothing had changed. Eventually it will be just a house and we will be forced to move on. But for now, it is still hers. It is still the home my grandfather designed and built, imbued with the lives of 3 generations under its simple roof and stone walls.

I wonder how much longer it will be there, the property shared amongst four siblings. It has already been threatened before, the state first offering, then greedily taking the surrounding land of which were once woods and gardens to build towering apartment complexes. Even before her death, the ephemeral nature of this once magical place of my childhood had revealed itself. Without proper care, her gardens lost their pristine beauty and grew untamed over time. The couch swing on which I quietly spent afternoons with my grandfather, filled with dirt and rain, growing moldy and unusable. Her beautiful black car which had never lost its new car small rarely left the gates with nobody to drive it, nowhere to go.

The family tree on my mothers' side is slowly contracting before my eyes and I fear that it will soon be her turn. But there is still so much that I don't know, either lost in translation in the move between countries or to the folds and cracks of time. My mental picture is snippets and pieces but that is not enough to go off of. It is not enough to pass down if I ever decided to start my own family. But how do you get to know someone when they are already gone and you struggle to communicate with those that are left to tell you about them? When their personal items remain in a country seven thousand miles away boxed up somewhere under a sloping attic? Sometimes it is easier to admit defeat, to cry, to mourn the challenge without putting up a fight.

But crying will get me nowhere. It will not reverse time or return what is lost. Little by little I must remember. I remember my grandfather's painting that hangs in our kitchen, his artworks proudly displayed around my grandmother's house. I remember her stylish pantsuits and blazers that now hang in the back of my closet. All is not yet lost. Perhaps insignificant, perhaps incomplete, there are still pieces to a puzzle that are lodged in the depths of my brain. There are surviving fragments that remain despite their crumbling foundation. And most importantly, I am not an island. I still have access to one last line of defense, who holds more stories, more information than any singular item or collection. The chain may be rusty but still it holds, it holds me tight.

Emily Bunch—My Mom, Her Best Friend, and Me

Sherry and Laura were here. That was the name of the book they were going to write. It would have been about their lives as best friends. A collection of their stories. Sherry was my mom. Laura was her best friend.

As the time in-between the present and my mother's death stretches farther and farther and I fight to keep the stories she would tell me fresh, there is one that I can still here her telling me today.

The stories about her and Laura. She and Laura met when they were in 8th grade at the same middle school, I went to too. They once snuck out the window at their chorus concert rehearsal and went and walked around the village of our town. At some point later on in their friendship, they spray painted "Sherry and Laura were here" under the bridge in that same village. They never lived it down. Well into their 40s, they still thought they were so cool because they did that. Ever since those early years, for the rest of their lives, everyone knew that they were inseparable. Despite leading very different lives as adults, they still somehow found ways to intertwine them. When Laura broke her foot and had surgery, my mom insisted that she stay at our house because my Mom would have worried too much. When my Mom was taking me to an away sports competition alone, Laura decided she would come too. They really never changed from the stories my mom told me of them always walking through their high school halls together. They laughed about some of their differences, and cried about others, but I always remember them being there for each other no matter the circumstances.

Their friendship was the first example in my life of female friendship, and of platonic love, two things that I have turned to for strength after they both have passed. My mom passed away first. I have always felt a sharp sting of sadness when I think about the fact that Laura had to learn a life without Sherry, because that was never their plan. After Laura passed away years later, I struggled to find a spot in between the feeling of peace that they were together again, and the lump in my throat that reminded me that one of the last and most important pieces of my mom's life was gone. I now had two laughs to try to remember. I hope I never forget them. Sometimes in my head I pretend that I am playing a game to see how long I can go on living without them. It helps to get me by.

There is one physical thing I have that will always remind me of the two of them. Laura gave it to me after my mom had passed away. It is a hat, and it is red. I pretty much misplace everything, but I have always been careful not to lose it. It is from a Kenny Chesney concert that they went to together at some point, one of many. Laura said she got the hat, but my mom always wanted it, and she gave it to me.

I wish I could call them both and see their faces when I tell them how many concerts I have been to now. I think I might just have them beat.

This hat is a physical reminder of the way they both impacted my life, and the person I am today. They loved to have fun, which is why they found themselves at this Kenny Chesney concert. Nearly all of my memories of them together involve them laughing. A huge testament to their friendship; the only times they were not laughing were when they were crying. And even sometimes the two were simultaneous.

I have always loved music, and this hat serves as a reminder for where that came from, my mom. She was the first person to realize how much I loved music when I was 4 years old, and took me to my first concert, Taylor Swift. The understanding my mom had for my interests ultimately ended up saving me later on in life. My love for music flows through the two holes in my heart for both of them. They will never be filled until I am with the two of them again, but for now I am okay.

They say you can't change the cards you are dealt, but you can play them. And God have I played them. Since the last time I got to be in the same room as my mom and Laura, I have chased my love for music wherever it let me go. Recently, I flew to Florida solely to see Taylor Swift with my best friend, and last summer we drove 6 hours to go to a music festival Kid Cudi was playing at. I have truly lived out my little music loving dreams. I am bad at counting, but I would estimate that I have been to over 100 concerts in the last two years, through cities, and states, through different friendships, through the grounds of music festivals, and ultimately through my years growing up. I have run away to a life I am okay with living, and I think that is something you are forced to learn about grief. At some point you run so far you can't imagine what it would be like to have them back. The distance breeds a startling sense of discomfort, but also a feeling of peace that you are okay for now. Sometimes, guilt creeps in wreaking havoc on my newfound composure. I instead fight to allow my love for this part of my life to serve as a comfort in place of the love I would receive if they were here.

Sometimes, I feel like my love for music allows me to make up for the parts of my childhood I lost to grief. Sometimes, the experiences music has given me make me almost okay with all the terrible parts of life I have had to live although, I mourn my childhood as I mourn my mother. The death of my mother and the death of my childhood interact in strange ways, and I fight to shield myself with memories. I begin to forget the color of my childhood bike as I try to remember her teaching me to ride the bike. The memories of my childhood, and my memories of my mom, and Laura too, fight aggressively for space in my brain. Little by little, I lose them.

But the truth is, I must grow up and farther away from them, timewise. Every day of my life, I try to reason with this internal conflict. I instead choose to focus on the gains, the good parts. Despite not being able to now share my love for music with my mom, I have gotten to share it with so many other people because of the course my life has taken. The path that grief led me down ultimately showed me a way to connect with people, through music. This Sunday, I am driving 6 hours to go to yet another Taylor Swift concert in Boston. And on Sunday, I will stand in the stadium where I saw Taylor Swift with my mom for the last time, this time, with my best friend. Would she be my best friend, and would I be doing this, if my life went perfectly and I never experienced loss?

Probably not. Would I be driving 6 hours to go to a concert? Absolutely not.

But that is the last thing I will say about grief; I have learned to always chase what I love instead of sitting back in fear that I will lose it. Trying to find a comfortable spot in between the parts of my life I am so in love with, and the heartbreak that sits behind that love reminding me that my mom and Laura are not there to sit back and watch this, probably laughing, is one of the hardest things I have ever done.

But I'll be okay for now with my hat. And as I said if I lose everything, but I will never lose that hat.

Cassandra Hughes—Single-Use Plastics and Lifetime Guilt

Waste. Garbage. Trash. Something we all produce daily, have to deal with daily, and yet we shy away from conversation about it. I for one have spent a great deal of my life contemplating and tormenting over how much garbage I was creating. At twenty-one years old I believe it is impossible to live a genuinely sustainable lifestyle while being a contributing and well-adjusted member of western society. It is a great privilege to worry about the environment let alone take measures to limit your plastic usage and be able to afford reusable materials. I've become a cynic when it comes to the state of the environment; nothing will change for the better unless large corporations themselves actually take action to reverse their damage and turn around their production practices. On one side of the spectrum this makes me feel slightly better about myself; at least I'm not killing the planet as much as Shein right? But on the other end I have this feeling that due to the sheer driving force of capitalism and the eternal greed of all things convenience-things probably won't ever look better than this. We all know our habits aren't sustainable, but I, like many others, can acknowledge this fact: Why should I try so damn hard if the people responsible are not? It's selfish and it sucks and a part of me doesn't even want to have kids because I alone hate that I was born at this point in time of irreversible pollution. I can just imagine it, taking my beautiful little baby for her yearly doctor's checkup and the pediatrician tells me my kid is full of microplastics.

I think I cared a lot more about my environmental impact when I had less of an understanding of the world. Not to say that I don't care now, but I'm much more cynical towards the state of the world and the environment than I was when I was 16 and had an infinite amount of time on my hands to blame others. I'll admit I was an asshole. I'm not proud of it, but it was coming from a place of existential dread like I was at fault for the world ending. I went fully vegan at 13, carried reusable utensils in my backpack at all times, took reusable straws and cups to coffee shops, and had reusable bags for my family's groceries. I projected so much of this onto my mom as well. She switched to biodegradable toilet paper for my family, jars for all of our dried foods such as beans, lentils etc. When back to school shopping came around my senior year of high school, my best friend and I felt so guilty for just the sheer amount of plastic we had to buy from our pens, folders, and etc. At 18 years old I felt *guilty* for using a pen—god forbid I needed it for my statistics homework. My best friend even made a joke that we should bring feather ink pens to school like the founding fathers.

I remember the sheer panic of realizing how much waste I was producing by wearing contact lenses. My eye doctor told me my eyes were too sensitive for monthlies so he highly recommended I wear dailies. My parents would scold me for letting the empty contact containers stack up in my bathroom. If I didn't throw them out, they wouldn't be considered waste, so they stacked up like a physical reminder and metaphor of the waste I had no control over creating, no matter how hard I tried in other facets of life.

This obsession ended when I found this online generator where you input how many years you'd been vegan and it would tell you how many animals you'd "saved" and how many gallons of water you have preserved. I hadn't even "saved" a whole cow in 7 years. My contact lenses kept stacking up, all coffee stops stopped allowing reusable cups to be used during the Pandemic, and my family began having to buy much more single use plastics than ever before because we weren't able to go to the grocery store. Worrying about contact lenses and how many water bottles I'd used in my lifetime began to feel stupid. Seven days a week, two pairs of lenses a day, 14 contact lenses a day, 56 containers a month, 672 contact containers a year. You can't fit 672 contact lenses into a mason jar like the dumb minimalist, low waste YouTubers I watched in middle school that corrupted my brain to think like this.

One coffee a day, 365 plastic cups a year, 365 plastic straws. At what point do you separate the necessities of actually enjoying your life and the crippling guilt of feeling like you're responsible for the world ending. Corporations produce nearly all of the waste produced worldwide, there's nothing I could do to offset this. I could live my entire life obsessively and miserably carrying the weight of pollution on my back, or I could just get the coffee, wear my contacts, and order the takeout without guilt. Takeout once a week, one Styrofoam container a week, 52 Styrofoam containers a year. There are landfills serving as graveyards of my greediness, laziness, and lack of care. I wonder how it would feel to visually see a lifetime of waste produced by one person—would my consciousness feel defeated? Would I still feel like I'm better than others for filling up my water bottle?

I think I wear my clothes out more than most people I know. I like that rugged worn out look to my coats and outerwear. Friends of mine throw out clothes in perfectly good condition and I even had a roommate once who threw her sweatshirts in the trash anytime the fabric began to pill. There's nothing wrong with slightly worn fabric and it's even comfier for lounging around clothes so this, naturally, pissed me off. My parents have a habit of buying more food than they can eat before it goes bad, and I feel very guilty that I haven't been able to shake out this habit on my own. It's hard buying groceries for one—I think I can eat all that produce in a week but I'm barely home and by the time I open my fridge on the weekends my strawberries have grown mold and my lettuce smells funky. This habit alone makes me feel like an asshole when I see people struggling to just make ends meet. I've gotten a lot better since I began living on my own, but inherently being wasteful is in my nature.

At the end of the day so much of sustainability and ethical preaching is a way for companies and brands to market themselves into seeming more environmentally friendly despite the truth of not being ethical in the slightest. Some of the best ways to reduce waste I've learned is to just wear the clothes you have, eat as many leftovers as possible, reuse things when you can, and to donate and pass on hand me downs to the best of your ability. The plastic will be made no matter what you do; it'll end up in the landfill whether you're the one using it or not. I have a lot of respect for people who dedicate their whole lives to low waste management and environmental activism, but along with all of that comes so much fear mongering and shaming others. I don't think that's fair to put onto others, especially since I as a child had these people negatively impact how I viewed the world and say that I was responsible for it.

BIBLIOGRAPHY

Adams, Tony E., Stacy Holman Jones, and Carolyn Ellis (2001), *Autoethnography*, New York: Oxford University Press.

Adams, Tony E., Stacy Holman Jones, and Carolyn Ellis, eds. (2013), *Handbook of Autoethnography*, Walnut Creek: Left Coast Press.

Atwood, Margaret (1990), "The Female Body," *Michigan Quarterly Review*, 29 (4): 491–3.

Barnett, Scot and Casey Boyle, eds. (2016), *Rhetoric, Through Everyday Things*, 2nd ed., Chicago: U Alabama Press.

Baudrillard, Jean (1996), *The System of Objects*, London: Verso.

Bédat, Maxine (2021), *Unraveled: The Life and Death of a Garment*, New York: Portfolio / Penguin.

Benjamin, Walter (1968), *Illuminations*, New York: Schocken.

Benson, Sophie (2023), "Should You Buy from a Thrift Store If You Can Afford Not To?," *British Vogue*, February 25. Available online: https://www.vogue.co.uk/fashion/article/is-thrifting-ethical (accessed January 5, 2025).

Brown, Bill (2004), *A Sense of Things: The Object Matter of American Literature*, Chicago: U Chicago Press.

Brickell, Chris and Judith Collard, eds. (2019), *Queer Objects*, New Brunswick: Rutgers.

Chitrakorn, Kati (2022), "The Fight for the Fashion Archive: Brands, Collectors and Gen Z Face Off," *Vogue*, April 27. Available online: https://www.voguebusiness.com/fashion/the-fight-for-the-fashion-archive-anna-sui-pucci-brands-gen-z-face-off (accessed January 5, 2025).

Didion, Joan (1968), *Slouching Towards Bethlehem*, New York: Farrar, Straus and Giroux.

Dillard, Annie (1998), "To Fashion a Text," in William Zinsser (ed.), *Inventing the Truth: The Art and Craft of Memoir*, 141–61, Boston: Mariner.

Eichorn, Kate (2014), *The Archival Turn in Feminism: Outrage in Order*, Ann Arbor: American Literatures Initiative.

Ellis, Carolyn (2013), "Preface," in Adams, Tony E., Stacy Holman Jones, and Carolyn Ellis (eds.), *Handbook of Autoethnography*, 9–12, Walnut Creek: Left Coast Press.

Fowles, Severin (2010), "People Without Things," in Mikkel Bille, Frida Hastrup, and Tim Flohr Soerensen (eds.), *An Anthropology of Absence: Materializations of Transcendence and Loss*, 23–41, Berlin: Springer Nature.

Gay, Roxane (2014), *Bad Feminist: Essays*, New York: Harper Perennial.

Gerber, Marisa (2021), "COVID-19 Took Away Their Last Moments Together. Now Families Cherish What Was Left Behind," *The Los Angeles Times*, April 30. Available online: https://www.latimes.com/california/story/2021-04-30/after-covid-deaths-families-cherish-items-from-loved-ones (accessed January 5, 2025).

Gibson, Margaret (2008), *Objects of the Dead: Mourning and Memory in Everyday Life*, Victoria: Melbourne University Press.

Greenberg, Reesa, Bruce W. Ferguson and Sany Nairne, eds. (1996), *Thinking About Exhibitions*, London: Routledge.

Guruianu, Andrei and Natalia Andrievskikh (2018), *The Afterlife of Discarded Objects: Memory and Forgetting in a Culture of Waste*, Anderson: Parlor Press.

Gutkind, Lee (1996), "The Five Rs of Creative Nonfiction," *Creative Nonfiction* 6 (4). Available online: https://creativenonfiction.org/writing/the-5-rs-of-creative-nonfiction/ (accessed January 5, 2025).

Hawkins, Gay and Stephen Muecke, eds. (2002), *Culture and Waste: The Creation and Destruction of Value*, Lanham: Rowman & Littlefield.

Holman Jones, Stacy, Tony E. Adams, and Carolyn Ellis (2013), "Introduction: Coming to Know Autoethnography as More than a Method," in Tony E. Adams, Stacy Holman Jones, and Carolyn Ellis, (eds.), *Handbook of Autoethnography*, 17–47, Walnut Creek: Left Coast Press.

HISTORY.com editors (2006), "Oprah Winfrey Confronts Author James Frey Over Lying," *History.com*, January 26. Available online: https://www.history.com/this-day-in-history/oprah-winfrey-takes-james-frey-to-task-for-lying (accessed January 5, 2025).

Hobbs, Margo (2019), "The Cunt Coloring Book," in Chris Brickell and Judith Collard (eds.), *Queer Objects*, 118–21, New Brunswick: Rutgers.

Hollander, John (1995), *The Gazer's Spirit: Poems Speaking to Silent Works of Art*, Chicago: U of Chicago Press.

Jimerson, Randall C. (2009), *Archives Power: Memory, Accountability and Social Justice*, Chicago: Society of American Archivists.

Karr, Mary (2015), *The Art of Memoir*, New York: HarperCollins.

Kilgannon, Corey (2025), "Bob Dylan is Having a Hollywood Moment. His No. 1 Hater is Ready," *New York Times*, January 14. Available online: https://www.nytimes.com/2025/01/10/nyregion/bob-dylan-nemesis.html (accessed January 15, 2025).

Kitchen, Judith and Mary Paumier Jones, eds. (1996), *In Short: A Collective of Brief Creative Nonfiction*, New York: WW Norton.

Kondo, Marie (2014), *The Life-changing Magic of Tidying Up: The Japanese Art of Decluttering and Organizing*, Berkeley: Ten Speed Press.

Maguire, John (2012), "The Secret to Good Writing: It's About Objects, Not Ideas," *The Atlantic*, October 2. Available online: https://www.theatlantic.com/national/archive/2012/10/the-secret-to-good-writing-its-about-objects-not-ideas/263113/ (accessed January 5, 2025).

Morrison, Toni (1998), "The Site of Memory," in William Zinsser (ed.), *Inventing the Truth: The Art and Craft of Memoir*, 183–200, Boston: Mariner.

Object lessons (2025), "About." Available online: https://objectsobjectsobjects.com/about/ (accessed January 5, 2025).

Parms, Jericho (2016), *Lost Wax: Essays*, Atlanta: U Georgia Press.

Peabody, Richard and Lucinda Ebersole, eds. (1993). *Mondo Barbie: An Anthology of Fiction and Poetry*, New York: St. Martin's Press.

Potts, Rolf (2018), *Souvenirs* (Object Lessons), London: Bloomsbury Academic.

Reilly, Maura (2018), *Curatorial Activism: Towards an Ethics of Curating*, London: Thames & Hudson.

Ro, Christine (2017), "A Birth Certificate Is a Person's First Possession," *The Atlantic*, December 10. Available online: https://www.theatlantic.com/technology/archive/2017/12/a-birth-certificate-is-a-persons-first-possession/547970/ (accessed January 5, 2025).

Russo, Naomi (2017), "The Still Misunderstood Shape of the Clitoris," *The Atlantic*, March 9. Available online: https://www.theatlantic.com/health/archive/2017/03/3d-clitoris/518991/ (accessed January 5, 2025).

Schneider, Pat (2003), *Writing Alone and with Others*, New York: Oxford U Press.

Schwartz, Mimi (1998), "Memoir? Fiction? Where's the Line?," *Creative Nonfiction* 10. Available online: https://creativenonfiction.org/writing/memoir-fiction-wheres-the-line/ (accessed January 5, 2025).

Steketee, Gail and Randy O. Frost (2011), *Stuff: Compulsive Hoarding and the Meaning of Things*, Boston: Mariner.

Suleiman, Susan Rubin (2007), "The Silver Pin," in Sherry Turkle (ed.), *Evocative Objects: Things We Think With*, 185–92, Cambridge: MIT Press.

Sullivan, Nikki and Craig Middleton (2019), "Bloomers and Monocles," in Chris Brickell and Judith Collard (eds.), *Queer Objects*, 326–9, New Brunswick: Rutgers.

Temporary Services (2022), *Book Waste Book*, Chicago: Half Letter Press.

Thomas, Dana (2019), *Fashionopolis: The Price of Fast Fashion and the Future of Clothes*, New York: Penguin.

Tombro, Melissa (2016), *Teaching Autoethnography: Personal Writing in the Classroom*, Geneseo: Open SUNY Textbooks.

Townsend, Mary (2018), "Throw Your Children's Art Away," *The Atlantic*, September 16. Available online: https://www.theatlantic.com/family/archive/2018/09/throw-your-childrens-art-away/570379/ (accessed January 5, 2025).

Turkle, Sherry (2007), *Evocative Objects: Things We Think With*, Cambridge: MIT Press.

Wiesenthal, Christine (2016), "Material Culture and Creative Writing Pedagogy: A Case for 'Garbage Land' (in real time and space)," *New Writing* 13 (2): 194–203.

Yaeger, Patricia (2002), 'Trash as Archive, Trash as Enlightenment,' in Gay Hawkins and Stephen Muecke (eds.), *Culture and Waste: The Creation and Destruction of Value*, 103–16, Lanham: Rowman & Littlefield.

Zinsser, William ed. (1998), *Inventing the Truth: The Art and Craft of Memoir*, Boston: Mariner.

INDEX

acquisition 45–7
activism 75
  Yaeger, Patricia 126
Adams, Tony E. 67, 70
Andrievskikh, Natalia 127–8
antiques 39, 47–50, 83
archives 86–92, 100–8
  assignment, high stakes 104–5
    student writing 106–8, 166–79
  assignment, low stakes 100–1, 103
    student writing 101–2, 165
  business 97–9
  curation 87–92
  digital 91–2
  Eichorn, Kate 89–91
  Fashion Institute of Technology 86–7
  feminist archives 89–92
  Freedman, Jenna 91
  Jimerson, Randall C. 87–8
  Lesbian Herstory Archives 89–92
  New York Public Library 88–9
  Trivette, Karen 86–7
assignments, high stakes 33–6; *see also* high stakes assignments
  essay #1 Collections 34–6, 58–60
    student writing 60–3, 149–61
  essay #2 Institutional Collections 104–5
    student writing 106–8, 166–79
  essay #3 The Things Left Behind 132–3
    student writing 134–7, 184–93
assignments, low stakes 32–3; *see also* low stakes assignments
  assignment #1 Bedroom Objects 22–3, 25, 71
    student writing 23–4, 147–8
  assignment #2 Collecting 56
    student writing 57–8, 148–9
  assignment #4 Gendered Objects 79–80
    student writing 80–2, 161–5
  assignment #5 Institutional Objects 100–1
    student writing 101–2, 165
  assignment #6 Archive Questions 103
  assignment #8 Trash 128–9
    student writing 129–30, 180–2
  assignment #9 Reduce, Reuse, Recycle! 130–1
    student writing 131–2, 182–4
Atwood, Margaret 76–7
authorial voice 27
autoethnography 65–83
  Adams, Tony E. 67, 70
  assignment, low stakes 79–80
    student writing 80–2, 161–5
  definition 65–8

Ellis, Carolyn 66–67, 70
gender 73–82
Holman Jones, Stacy 67, 70
interview 71–3
keepsakes 68–70
observation 71–3
research 68–70
Tombro, Melissa 3–4, 65–6, 72–3

Barbie dolls 42–3
Duhamel, Denise 42
Ebersole, Lucinda 42
Peabody, Richard 42
Barnard Zine Library 89–92
Freedman, Jenna 91
Baudrillard, Jean 43–4
Bédat, Maxine 118
Benjamin, Walter 44–5
Benson, Sophie 112
birth certificates 14
bookmaking 126
Branding; *see* businesses
Brickell, Chris 74–5
broken objects 124–5
mending 125
Brown, Bill 52–4
Bruner, Mia 89
businesses 97–108

Chicago, Judy 76
Chitrakorn, Kati 97–8
clitoris 74
Russo, Naomi 74
Collard, Judith 74–5
collections, institutional 83–109
assignment, high stakes 104–5
student writing 106–8, 166–79
assignment, low stakes 100–1, 103
student writing 101–2, 165
Barnard Zine Library 89–92
business 97–108
curation 87–92
digital 91–2
Fashion Institute of Technology 86–7
feminist archives 89–92
Judd, Donald 84
Lesbian Herstory Archives 89–92
The Lever House 99
New York Public Library 88–9
Tiffany & Co. 98–9
collections, personal 39–64
assignment, high stakes 34–6, 58–60
student writing 60–3, 149–61
assignment, low stakes 56
student writing 57–8, 148–9
Barbie dolls 42–3
Baudrillard, Jean 43–4
Benjamin, Walter 44–5
Brown, Bill 52–4
definition 39–41
Duhamel, Denise 42
Ebersole, Lucinda 42
hoarding 50–4, 58–9, 84
human touch 84–5, 113–16
minimalism 54–6, 58–9
Potts, Rolf 14–15
pursuit 45–50
souvenirs 14–15
valuation 41–5
consistency 27
Corinne, Tee A. 75
COVID 115–16
Gerber, Marisa 115–16
creative nonfiction pedagogy 7–37
assignment, low stakes 22–3, 25, 71
student writing 23–4, 147–8
audience 26–7
authorial voice 27
choosing topics 24–5
conclusions 31–2
consistency 27
context 25–9

dialogue 29–31
five senses 28–30
freewriting 7
Gutkind, Lee 71
Kitchen, Judith 11–12
Maguire, John 14
Morrison, Toni 18
Paumier Jones, Mary 11–12
revision/workshop 32–6
Schneider, Pat 32–3
setting the scene 19, 28–30
titling 31–2
trust 16–17
truth 17–20
Turkle, Sherry 13
Wiesenthal, Christine 124
The Cunt Coloring Book 75
Corinne, Tee A. 75

death 113–16
assignment, high stakes 132–3
student writing 134–7, 184–91
Gerber, Marisa 115–16
Gibson, Margaret 113–15
museum 40, 84
O'Brien, Tim 116
Suleiman, Susan Rubin 69–70
television 55
Didion, Joan 18
Dillard, Annie 19–20
Dodson, Betty 75
donations 113–14
Duhamel, Denise 42

Ebersole, Lucinda 42
Edel, Deborah 90
Eichorn, Kate 89–91
Ellis, Carolyn 66–67, 70
Bédat, Maxine 118
business archives 97–9
fashion 46, 76–8, 118, 125
Fashion Institute of Technology archives 86–7
fast fashion 111–12, 117–18
Japanese Sashiko 125
Middleton, Craig 76
Sullivan, Nikki 76
Thomas, Dana 11
Tiffany & Co. 98–9

female body 74–9
Atwood, Margaret 76–77
Ferguson, Bruce W. 93–4
Fowler, Ian 89
Fowles, Severin 10–11
Freedman, Jenna 91
freewriting 7
Frey, James 16
Frost, Randy O. 51–2, 84–5
Fundación Joan Miró 95

garbage; *see* trash
Gay, Roxane 77–8
gender 73–82
assignment, low stakes 79–80
student writing 80–2, 161–5
Atwood, Margaret 76–7
Brickell, Chris 74–5
Chicago, Judy 76
Collard, Judith 74–5
Corinne, Tee A. 75
The Cunt Coloring Book 75
Dodson, Betty 75
feminist archives 89–92
Gay, Roxane 77–8
Hobbs, Margo 75–6
Middleton, Craig 76
queer identity 74–6
Russo, Naomi 74
vulva 75–6
clitoris 74
Lesbian Herstory Archives LHA 89–92
Gerber, Marisa 115–16
Gibson, Margaret 113–15
Greenberg, Reesa 93–4
Guruianu, Andrei 127–8
Gutkind, Lee 71

Hawkins, Gay 118–19
high stakes assignments; *see also* assignments, high stakes
overview 33–6
hoarding 50–4, 58–9, 84
Frost, Randy O. 51–2, 84–5
Judd, Donald 84
Steketee, Gail 51–2, 84–5
Hobbs, Margo 75–6
Hollander, John 96
Holman Jones, Stacy 67, 70
hunt; *see* acquisition

Industrial Revolution 52–3
Brown, Bill 52–4
inheritance 68–9, 109–10, 113–16
collecting 42
hoarding, Collyer Brothers 50–1
Suleiman, Susan Rubin 69–70
interview 71–3

Japanese Sashiko 125
Jimerson, Randall C. 87–8
Judd, Donald 84

Karr, Mary 28–9
Keats, John 95–6
keepsakes 68–70
Kent Recycling Center 123
Kilgannon, Corey 120
Kitchen, Judith 11–12
Kondo, Marie 55

Lesbian Herstory Archives LHA 89–92
Edel, Deborah 90
The Lever House 99
low stakes assignments; *see also* assignments, low stakes
overview 32–3

Maguire, John 14
materiality 2, 10–11, 14
archives 86–87
Fowles, Severin 10–11
Materials for the Arts MFTA 122–3
memoir 16–20, 26–57
Didion, Joan 18
Dillard, Annie 19–20
Frey, James 16
Karr, Mary 28–9
Schwartz, Mimi 17–18
Tombro, Melissa 8–10, 47–50, 141–5
Metropolitan Museum of Art 93, 96–7, 105
Hollander, John 96
Middleton, Craig 76
minimalism 54–6, 58–9
Kondo, Marie 55
Morrison, Toni 18
Muecke, Stephen 118–19
museums 83–6, 92–7, 100–8
activism 94–5
assignment, high stakes 104–5
student writing 106–8
assignment, low stakes 99–100
student writing 101–2
Bringley, Patrick 96
curation 93–5
Ferguson, Bruce W. 93–4
Greenberg, Reesa 93–4
Hollander, John 96
Metropolitan Museum of Art 93, 96–7, 105
Nairne, Sany 93–4
Parms, Jericho 96–7
Reilly, Maura 94–5
student writing 101–2, 106–8, 165–79
Walker Art Center 95

Nairne, Sany 93–4
New York City 2–4, 14–15
Barnard Zine Library 89–92
Collyer Brothers 50–1
Edel, Deborah 90
Freedman, Jenna 91
inheritance 69

institutional collections 87, 91
Lesbian Herstory Archives
LHA 89–92
The Lever House 99
Materials for the Arts
MFTA 122–3
Metropolitan Museum of
Art 93, 96–7, 105
museums 92–3
New York Public Library 88–9
recycling 122
Tiffany & Co. 98–9
Tombro, Melissa 47–50
trash 110, 121–2
New York Public Library 88–9
Bruner, Mia 89
Fowler, Ian 89

object fixation 41–5
Object Lessons, *The Atlantic*
birth certificates 14
children's art 120–1
clitoris 74
materiality 14
overview 13–14
souvenirs 14–15
O'Brien, Tim 116
observation 71–3

Parms, Jericho 96–7
Paumier Jones, Mary 11–12
Peabody, Richard 42
pedagogy; *see* creative nonfiction
pedagogy
poetry 95–6
Hollander, John 96
Keats, John 95–6
Potts, Rolf 14–15

queer identity 74–6
Brickell, Chris 74–5
Collard, Judith 74–5
Middleton, Craig 76

recycling 122–8
recycling centers 123–4

Reilly, Maura 94–5
researching the self 68–70
Ro, Christine 40
Russo, Naomi 74

Schneider, Pat 32–3
Schwartz, Mimi 17–18
social media 12, 39–40, 46–7, 111
Every Outfit 46
Tiffany & Co. 97–8
souvenirs 14–15
Potts, Rolf 14–15
Steketee, Gail 51–2, 84–5
student writing
Bunch, Emily 180–1, 188–91
De Paz, Maximiliano 134–7,
163–4
Dery, Renée 80–2, 153–7
Diop, Amy 57–8, 165, 181–2
Duffett, Hailey 23–4, 148–9
Hughes, Cassandra 157–61,
191–3
Krupa, Scott 161–3, 169–72
Lapointe, David 147–8
Loose, Sarah 106–8
Magliulo, Krystal 173–9
Stratton, Lyla 131–2
Urbina, Maya 164–5
Walicke, Alexandra 101–2,
182–4
Wicks, Eliza 129–30, 166–9,
184–8
Suleiman, Susan Rubin 69–70
Sullivan, Nikki 76

television 46–7, 50, 55, 125
American Pickers 46–7, 50
Antiques Road Trip 46–7
Hoarders 50
Sex and the City 46
Swedish Death Cleaning 55
The Repair Shop 125
Temporary Services 126
Thomas, Dana 11
thrifting 111–12
Benson, Sophie 112

Tiffany & Co. 98–9
titling 31–2
Tombro, Melissa
  autoethnography 65–6, 72–3
  memoir 8–10, 47–50, 144–5
Townsend, Mary 120–1
choosing a topic 24–5
trash 109–12
  Andrievskikh, Natalia 127–8
  art 126–7
  assignment, high stakes 132–3
    student writing 134–7, 184–93
  assignments, low stakes 128–31
    student writing 129–30, 180–2
  Bédat, Maxine 118
  bookmaking 126
  broken objects 124–5
  children 120–1
  cultural values 117–21, 127–8
  emotion 118–20
  Guruianu, Andrei 127–8
  Hawkins, Gay 118–19
  Kilgannon, Corey 120
  Materials for the Arts MFTA 122–3
  mending 125
  Muecke, Stephen 118–19
  overview 110–11
  personal trash 120–1
  recycling 122–8
  repurposing 126–8
  textiles 111
  Townsend, Mary 120–1
  trash audits 121–2
  upcycling 111, 122–3, 125, 127–8
  Vonnegut, Kurt 121
  Wiesenthal, Christine 124
  Yaeger, Patricia 126
trash audits 121–2
Trivette, Karen 86–7
truth 17–20
  Morrison, Toni 18
Turkle, Sherry 13

University of Illinois Urbana-Champaign archives 87
upcycling 111, 122–3, 125–8
  art 126–7
  assignment, low stakes 130–1
    student writing 131–2, 182–4
  bookmaking 126
  culture 127–8
  Materials for the Arts MFTA 122–3

Vonnegut, Kurt 121
vulva 75–6
  Hobbs, Margo 75–6

Walker Art Center 95
waste; *see* trash
Wiesenthal, Christine 124

Yaeger, Patricia 126